PORTFOLIO / PENGUIN

WHAT THE MOST SUCCESSFUL PEOPLE DO BEFORE BREAKFAST

LAURA VANDERKAM is the author of *168 Hours: You Have More Time Than You Think*; *All the Money in the World: What the Happiest People Know About Getting and Spending*; *What the Most Successful People Do Before Breakfast*; *What the Most Successful People Do on the Weekend*; and *What the Most Successful People Do at Work*. Her work has appeared in *The Wall Street Journal*, *The Huffington Post*, *USA Today*, *Scientific American*, and *Reader's Digest*, among other publications. She lives outside Philadelphia with her husband and their three children.

Visit lauravanderkam.com

Want more time management tips and advice?
Please scan this code to sign up for Laura's monthly newsletter.

LAURA
VANDERKAM

WHAT THE MOST SUCCESSFUL PEOPLE DO BEFORE BREAKFAST

AND TWO OTHER SHORT
GUIDES TO ACHIEVING
MORE AT WORK AND
AT HOME

PORTFOLIO / PENGUIN

PORTFOLIO / PENGUIN
Published by the Penguin Group
Penguin Group (USA), 375 Hudson Street,
New York, New York 10014, USA

USA | Canada | UK | Ireland | Australia | New Zealand | India | South Africa | China
Penguin Books Ltd, Registered Offices: 80 Strand, London WC2R 0RL, England
For more information about the Penguin Group visit penguin.com

First published by Portfolio/Penguin, a member of Penguin Group (USA), 2013

What the Most Successful People Do Before Breakfast (2012), *What the Most
Successful People Do on the Weekend* (2012), and *What the Most Successful People
Do at Work* (2013) first published in electronic book format by Penguin Group
(USA).

LIBRARY OF CONGRESS CATALOGING-IN-PUBLICATION DATA
Vanderkam, Laura.
What the most successful people do before breakfast : and two other short guides
to achieving more at work and at home / Laura Vanderkam.
  pages cm
ISBN 978-1-59184-669-7 (pbk.)
1. Time management.   2. Success in business.   3. Success.   I. Title.
HD69.T54V363 2013
650.1—dc23
2013019885

Printed in the United States of America
10   9

Set in Minion Pro
Designed by Neuwirth & Associates, Inc

While the author has made every effort to provide accurate telephone numbers,
Internet addresses, and other contact information at the time of publication,
neither the publisher nor the author assumes any responsibility for errors, or for
changes that occur after publication. Further, publisher does not have any control
over and does not assume any responsibility for author or third-party Web sites or
their content.

CONTENTS

INTRODUCTION

Though you have just picked up a physical book, *What the Most Successful People Do Before Breakfast* was born in the digital world.

My first book on time management, *168 Hours*, came out in May 2010. Shortly after that, I started blogging a few times a week for BNET (an entity later folded into CBS *MoneyWatch*) on time management topics. Every morning I got traffic reports from the previous day. I found this feedback both addictive and inspiring. Studying the data, I began to see what topics and titles most interested people. I could also see which posts got the digital equivalent of a shrug.

One day in May 2011, I found myself writing about one of my favorite bits of time management advice: using your mornings well. Over the years I'd noticed that people who get a lot done tend to make use of these hours that the rest of us fail to seize. While some of us hit snooze, they're training for half marathons. While some of us struggle to get our kids dressed and out the door, they have fun family breakfasts and organize their little ones into morning book clubs. I wrote about activities one could do in the early hours, before life has the chance to get away from you. Then I sat there trying to figure out a title. I thought about calling the post "Use Your Mornings Well." But at the last moment, with those traffic reports buzzing around in my brain, I changed that to "What the Most Successful People Do Before Breakfast."

It turned out to be a smart move. Something about that title drew readers in. We all want to be successful, but changing how we spend the entire 168 hours we all have each week seems daunting. Changing what we do before breakfast? That sounds doable. My traffic data soon soared—spiking into the six figures on one memorable day—as people shared the link around the Internet.

Traffic drifted back to earth after a week or so, but whenever I'd include that title in lists of links, it would get another spike. I realized I had stumbled onto an idea that people really cared about. But what should I do with that knowledge?

That fall, I went to a book party in New York for another Portfolio author. While there, I chatted with my editor, Brooke Carey, who had told me in the past of Penguin's desire to experiment more with the e-book market. E-readers and tablet computers were changing the field of publishing, and all of us were trying to figure out what would work. E-books could be any length, and the sweet spot of roughly ten thousand to fifteen thousand words (readable on a train commute) seemed perfect for fleshing out my ideas on creating better mornings. I suggested publishing *What the Most Successful People Do Before Breakfast* in the format that Penguin was then calling an "e-special." Within a few weeks we decided to make that happen. The e-book came out in June 2012, and the title worked its magic again. The audio version I'd recorded hit #1 for audiobooks on iTunes—briefly surpassing *Fifty Shades of*

Grey—and we decided to expand the concept into a series of e-books, looking at how successful people spend their weekends and workdays, too.

This paperback is a compilation of those e-books for people who still like to curl up with something that's got a cover and a spine. What experimenting with short e-books has taught me is that people want options. Sometimes we want to become absorbed in a topic—which a full-length book like this one allows—and sometimes we want a quick burst of motivation for the hard work of personal change. A short e-book can do that, and if you can read it before breakfast, all the better! In an era when technology personalizes everything it touches, why not interact with content however you'd like? To sweeten the deal on the printed version (which, as a bookworm, I confess I like best), I've also included a bonus section featuring time makeovers of people who wrote to me after reading my previous books. These readers wanted to change how they spent their early hours in order to make more of their mornings and their lives. The discovery? Crafting new habits is never easy. Still, over the course of several weeks, all these busy people made changes to their routines that they could live with.

I had a lot of fun writing these three short books. I interviewed fascinating people: CEOs, a presidential candidate, a bestselling children's book illustrator, a race car driver. I came across intriguing research on time use. And even though I've been writing about time management for years, I discovered lots of new ideas that I've been putting into practice in my own life. My family's weekends have certainly improved since we began putting more thought into them. Sunday night is my new favorite night for parties. I can't say I've become a morning person, but I'm trying to get to bed on time. And with the help of an accountability partner, I'm making progress on some projects I'd otherwise be tempted to chuck.

I hope you'll likewise find inspiration in here for making small tweaks that add up to big changes. I really do believe we can build the lives we want in the time we've got. Even a few minutes of strategizing before the rest of the world wakes up can make a day seem full of possibility—like an adventure, rather than a slog.

WHAT
THE MOST
SUCCESSFUL
PEOPLE

DO
BEFORE
BREAKFAST

THE MADNESS OF MORNINGS

Mornings are a madcap time in many households. Like mine. On mornings when I am responsible for getting my three children fed, dressed, and in the car by 8:45 a.m., I can be up before 7:00 and, if I'm not careful, feel like much of that time is spent dashing around. My eye is on the clock. I line up boots and coats to stave off last-minute disasters. Even so, it's always possible that one child will make a stand against some tyranny—like being forced to wear socks—and we inevitably cut things close at the end. After I drop them off at two different schools, I usually get back to my desk at around 9:15, when, instead of commencing my workday, I'm often tempted to just pour a cup of coffee and goof around online.

Having spent the past few years examining how people use their time, I know such orchestration—spending two or more hours each day getting ready to face what lies ahead—is nothing unusual. Magazines teem with stories on how to tame morning chaos. According to the National Sleep Foundation's 2011 Sleep in America poll, the average 30–45-year-old claims he or she gets out of bed at 5:59 on a typical weekday morning, with 46–64-year-olds rousting themselves at 5:57. Yet many people don't start work until 8:00 or 9:00 a.m. And by "start work" I mean "show up at the workplace." When people are frazzled from wrangling small children, battling traffic, or even standing in line for twenty minutes at Starbucks, it's easy to seize that first quiet stint at the office as unconsciously chosen me time. We read through personal e-mails and peruse Facebook and headlines totally unrelated to our jobs until a meeting or phone call forces us to stop.

In the end you can spend three to four hours a day on mindless tasks or barking at a petulant child to get in the car *now* or we are *driving off without you* instead of on your core competencies. These are your highest-value activities: nurturing your career, nurturing your family beyond basic personal care, and nurturing yourself. By that last category, I mean activities such as exercise, a hobby, meditation, prayer, and the like. The madness of mornings is a key reason most of us believe we have no time. We have time, but it's consumed by sound and fury that culminates in few accomplishments beyond getting out the door.

But mornings don't have to be like this. Studying my own, even on those madcap days, I see how they could be better. They can be productive times. Joyous times. Times for habits that help one grow into a better person. Indeed, learning to use mornings well is, in our distracted world, what separates achievement from madness. Before the rest of the world is eating breakfast, the most successful people have already scored daily victories that are advancing them toward the lives they want.

At least that's my conclusion from studying time logs and profiles in which high-achieving people talk about their schedules. Perusing the *Wall Street Journal* over coffee the other morning, I learned that while I was still sleeping, Rev. Al Sharpton had already done a workout. "He has a gym in his Upper West Side apartment building, where he's usually the only one working out when he arrives around 6:00 a.m.," the paper noted. He warms up for ten minutes on a stationary bike and jogs thirty minutes on a treadmill. Then it's on to the stability ball and crunches. "On days he can't get in his morning workout, he uses the gym at NBC Studios. He travels to two to three cities per week and says he makes his staff call ahead to ensure the hotel has a gym." Exercising in the wee hours, he never worries about what he looks like. "I usually wear an old track suit and Nikes," he told the *WSJ*. "It's so early no one sees me." Coupled with dietary changes, however, this early-morning ritual in grubby clothes has made the reverend look quite spiffy. He's lost more than one hundred pounds in the past few years.

James Citrin, who coleads the North American Board and CEO Practice at the headhunting firm Spencer Stuart, is also often exercising by 6:00 a.m. He uses that early-morning quiet to reflect on his most important priorities of the day. One day a few years ago, he decided to ask various executives he admired about their morning routines for a Yahoo! *Finance* piece. Of the eighteen (of twenty) who responded, the latest any of them was up regularly was 6:00 a.m. For instance, according to the interview notes Citrin later shared with me, Steve Reinemund, the former chairman and CEO of PepsiCo, was up at 5:00 a.m. and running four miles on the treadmill. Then he had some quiet time, praying and reading and catching up on the news, before eating breakfast with his then-teenage twins. When I asked Reinemund, currently the dean at Wake Forest University's Schools of Business, about his schedule, he said that he'd been running those four miles pretty much daily for decades. "I don't stay in a hotel that doesn't have a treadmill," he said. The exception to the routine? Sundays he starts a little later, and Thursdays he hosts "Dawn with the Dean," when Wake Forest students can meet him at 6:30 a.m. to run three miles.

Others of Citrin's survey respondents started even earlier. One executive told Citrin, "There is a diner in town (Louie's), where I go most every day for papers and coffee. . . . Opens at 4:30 a.m., have papers by 5:00 or so. . . . They know me there so when they see me through the front window it is time for Conway's large coffee and four papers. . . . Billy is usually behind the counter, and it is amazing how many regulars he can keep straight."

Whatever the ritual, though, there is a reason for these early-morning routines. Successful people have priorities they want to tackle, or things they like to do with their lives, and early mornings are the time when they have the most control of their schedules. In a world of constant connectivity, of managing global organizations, the day can quickly get away from you as other people's priorities invade—sometimes even those of the people you love dearly and share a home with. As I've been talking with people about their mornings, the phrase I hear repeated is that "this is the time I have for myself." As Reinemund told me, "I look forward to my mornings. I cherish my mornings, my personal time." An executive might never be able to relax in Louie's diner for an hour at 2:00 p.m., but at 5:00 in the morning, he can. I can't write in my journal quietly at 8:15 on those preschool mornings, or lift weights, but I can at 6:15. Parents can also use some of that breakfast time more consciously for nurturing our children, rather than keeping our eyes on the clock. Seizing your mornings is the equivalent of that sound financial advice to pay yourself before you pay your bills. If you wait until the end of the month to save what you have left, there will be nothing left over. Likewise, if you wait until the end of the day to do meaningful but not urgent things like exercise, pray, read, ponder how to advance your career or grow your organization, or truly give your family your best, it probably won't happen.

If it has to happen, then it has to happen first.

A MATTER OF WILLPOWER

If the world is filled with night owls and larks (like Reinemund, who reports that he was waking up at around 5:00 a.m. even as a student), I would be inclined to put myself in the former camp. In college I worked some late-night jobs like manning a café until 1:00 a.m. I studied then, too. Even after college when I got a "real" job, at *USA Today*, that required me to be up at a normal hour for an epic commute, I tended to do my creative work in the evenings. That was my habit, and I still like to work at that time on occasion. Ironic as it sounds, I wrote most of this missive—on what the most successful people do before breakfast—in a coffee shop at night.

Doing that at this stage of my life, however, with small children and work that more than fills normal business hours, required various logistical feats. I had to arrange additional babysitting coverage and answer to the smaller members of my family, who, quite reasonably, expected the hours after school and work to be family time. Consequently, these are not hours that I often take for focused work, let alone for exercise or other such pursuits.

And so I have begun to see the benefits of getting a jump on the day. We all have 168 hours a week, but not all hours are equally suited to all things. I certainly noticed this when I started tracking my time for my book on time management, *168 Hours*. As I kept time logs, writing down what I was doing as often as I remembered, I noticed patterns. Namely, during normal business hours, I would have one really good burst of productivity in the morning, when I could focus for ninety minutes or more on a single project. Later in the day, I became more easily distracted. Not only was I tempted to click over to e-mail or surf the Web, but things started piling up that I had to answer. I saw this on the time logs other people kept for me as well. As the day went on, the time spent on each individual task began to shrink.

As for exercise, I saw a few folks who managed to exercise after work, but these tended to be young, single sorts. Those of us who worked at home could squeeze in a workout during the day, since the lack of cubicle mates meant it didn't matter if we didn't shower afterward (or ever). But the sweat factor was a major deterrent to people with conventional jobs, as was the desire not to be seen walking out with a gym bag in the middle of the day, and the shockingly regular nature of work emergencies. Work hours had a way of stretching into evenings as deadlines loomed, and that planned workout never happened. People who were serious about exercise did it in the mornings. At that point, emergencies had yet to form, and they would have to shower only once. As Gordo Byrn, a triathlon coach, once told me, "There's always a reason to skip a four o'clock workout, and it's going to be a good reason, too."

Logistically, it makes sense that mornings are a good time for exercise or focused work, but as I made a few tune-ups based on my time logs and started pushing phone calls to the afternoon in order to take advantage of my morning productivity burst, I wondered if there were reasons beyond logistics that mornings seemed to be made for getting things done.

It turns out there are. New research into that old-fashioned concept of willpower is showing that tasks that require self-discipline are simply easier to do while the day is young.

Roy F. Baumeister, a professor of psychology at Florida State University, has spent his career studying this topic of self-discipline. In one famous experiment, he asked students to fast before coming in to the lab. Then they were put in a room, alone, with radishes, chocolate chip cookies, and candy. As Baumeister and science journalist John Tierney write in their 2011 book, *Willpower: Rediscovering the Greatest Human Strength*, some students could eat what they wanted, and some were assigned to eat only the radishes. Afterward, the participants had to work on unsolvable geometry puzzles. "The students who'd been allowed to eat chocolate chip cookies and candy typically worked on the puzzles for about twenty minutes, as did a control group of students who were also hungry but hadn't been offered food of any kind. The sorely tempted radish eaters, though, gave up in just eight minutes—a huge difference by the standards of laboratory experiments. They'd successfully resisted the temptation of the cookies and the chocolates, but the effort left them with less energy to tackle the puzzles."

What Baumeister and his colleagues took from this experiment is that "willpower, like a muscle, becomes fatigued from overuse." This is a problem because, while we think of our lives in categories like "work" and "home," the reality is that, as Baumeister told me, "You have one energy resource that is used for all kinds of acts for self-control. That includes not just resisting food temptations, but also controlling your thought processes, controlling your emotions, all forms of impulse control, and trying to perform well at your job or other tasks. Even more surprisingly, it is used for decision making, so when you make choices you are (temporarily) using up some of what you need for self-control. Hard thinking, like logical reasoning, also uses it." Over the course of a day, dealing with traffic, frustrating bosses, and bickering children, plus—more insidiously—electronic temptations that are as alluring as fresh-baked chocolate chip cookies, a person's supply of will-power is simply used up.

"There seems to be a general pattern that major self-control failures and other bad decisions occur late in the day," says Baumeister. "Diets are broken in the evening, not the morning. The majority of impulsive crimes are committed after 11:00 p.m. Lapses in drug use, alcohol abuse, sexual misbehavior, gambling excesses, and the like tend to come about late in the day."

In the morning, though, after a decent night's sleep, the supply of willpower is fresh. We're more inclined to be optimistic; one analysis of Twitter feeds from around the world found that people are more likely to use words like "awesome" and "super" between 6:00 and 9:00 a.m. than at other times of the day. In these early hours, we have enough willpower and energy to tackle things that require internal motivation, things the outside world does not immediately demand or reward— the things we'll get to later in this essay.

That's the argument for scheduling important priorities first. But there's more to the muscle metaphor. Muscles can be strengthened over time. A bodybuilder must work hard to develop huge biceps, but then he can go into maintenance mode and still look pretty buff. Paradoxically, with willpower, research has found that people who score high on measures of self-discipline tend not to employ this discipline when they do regular activities that would seem to require it, such as homework or getting to class or work on time. For successful people, these are no longer choices but habits. "Getting things down to routines and habits takes willpower at first but in the long run conserves willpower," says Baumeister. "Once things become habitual, they operate as automatic processes, which consume less willpower."

Take, for instance, brushing your teeth. Most of us don't stand there arguing with ourselves every morning about whether we want to brush, whether it's worth the effort of getting to the sink, whether the sensation of toothbrush bristles scrubbing around one's mouth is particularly pleasant. It's simply a morning ritual. Likewise, successful people turn high-value tasks into morning rituals, conserving their energy for later battles—those annoying colleagues, traffic, and other willpower sappers that make you want to drink a Mason jar full of wine in the evening rather than hit the gym. The jar of wine is still a bad idea, but if you do work out in the morning, at least you'll know you already hit the gym hours before if you decide to imbibe later. Through these daily habits, you make slow, steady progress—laying the foundation for happiness, health, and wealth. As Tierney and Baumeister write, "Ultimately, self-control lets you relax because it removes stress and enables you to conserve willpower for the important challenges."

IMPORTANT, BUT NOT
URGENT THINGS

So what are the best morning habits?

You can, of course, make a habit of anything you like. You could make a habit of doing laundry before most people are eating breakfast, or watching television before your children wake up. You could schedule a twenty-person conference call for that first precious hour of the workday. But most people don't need willpower to watch TV, and laundry tends to get done because it has to get done. Conference calls already rise to the top of the priority list (whether they deserve it or not) because they involve other people and show up on our schedules at certain times. The best morning rituals are activities that don't have to happen and certainly don't have to happen at a specific hour. These are activities that require internal motivation. The payoff isn't as immediate as the easy pleasure of watching television or answering an e-mail that doesn't require a speedy response, but there are still payoffs. The best morning rituals are activities that, when practiced regularly, result in long-term benefits.

The most successful people use their mornings for these things:

1. Nurturing their careers—strategizing and focused work
2. Nurturing their relationships—giving their families and friends their best
3. Nurturing themselves—exercise and spiritual and creative practices

We'll look at each in turn.

1. Nurturing Your Career

Debbie Moysychyn started a job in 2010 building a division of health-care education at Brandman University. She kept a time log as part of a workshop I did at the Healthcare Businesswomen's Association national convention and, after a few days of writing down what she was doing, she noted that "some things are painfully obvious!" Most notably, she kept getting interrupted. Her days were full of ad hoc meetings and short chats and thirty minutes on one thing and then thirty minutes on another. Part of this was by design. She was trying to establish a collaborative culture and had an open-door policy with her team. So, viewed from that perspective, these "interruptions" were the most important part of her day. The problem was that she had other projects she needed to do, too, and the disjointed nature of her schedule meant she never got very far.

The answer to this dilemma turned out to lie in a quirk of her personal life. Her teenage daughter played water polo and often needed to be in the pool well before 7:00 a.m. Sometimes after taking her, Moysychyn would go back home and watch TV, or she'd go in to the office and spend those early hours cleaning out her in-box. I noted that there were plenty of other times she could deal with her in-box—in those five-minute spurts between drop-in visits, for instance—but that no one was dropping into her office at 6:30 a.m. So that was a time for focused work. She could choose a top priority for each day, do that in the quiet wee hours, and then relax when colleagues visited her later on.

She agreed to give it a try and found the change pretty easy. She was already awake. She just had to make a habit of respecting this "project time" by not answering e-mails. A few days in, she told us at the workshop, she was getting so much done that she was sold. I checked in a few weeks later and learned that she was "still using early-morning time to do the heavy lifting." She told me, "I can accomplish more before breakfast than I used to do in a day. Maybe not quite, but I am checking long-standing things off my to-do list."

This lack of interruptions is a key reason that people cite for doing focused work early. You can crank things out; novelist Anthony Trollope famously wrote, without fail, for a few hours each morning. Charlotte Walker-Said, a history post-doc at the University of Chicago, uses the hours between 6:00 and 9:00 a.m. each day to work on a book on the history of religious politics in West Africa. She can read journal articles and write pages before dealing with her teaching responsibilities. "Once you start looking at e-mail, the whole day cascades into e-mail responses and replying back and forth," she says. These early-morning hours are key to managing her stress in a suboptimal academic job market. "Every day I have a job," she says, but "in the morning, I think I have a career." She's on to something; one study of young professors found that those who wrote a little bit every day were more likely to make tenure than those who wrote in bursts of intense energy (and put it off the rest of the time).

Of course, some people do find that dealing with the rest of the world in the morning works for them, particularly if they do it on their terms: sending e-mails that they need to think through and deciding on social media messages for the day. Gretchen Rubin, author of the bestselling book *The Happiness Project*, gets up at 6:00 a.m. so she has an hour to herself before the rest of her family gets up at 7:00. "I used to try to do heavy writing then, because I've read so often that people do their best thinking in the early part of the day," she says. "But after a year of frustration I realized that I need to spend an hour catching up with e-mail, social media, scheduling, and logistical things before I can settle down to concentrate—so now I use that 6:00–7:00 hour for that kind of work." She deems this ritual "very satisfying."

In that same vein of building a professional network, I've long thought that the "networking breakfast" concept is massively underappreciated. Parents and teetotalers often skip boozy cocktail parties, and even if you do attend, the presence of alcohol and the end-of-day mind-set means people are in social mode, not work mode. You forget to collect business cards, or you collect them and forget why you wished to speak to these people again. In the morning "people will roll up their sleeves and get to work," says Christopher Colvin, a partner at the law firm Kramer Levin Naftalis & Frankel, who often wakes up at 5:30 a.m. to walk the dog and read for work before giving his kids breakfast. To take advantage of that, he started IvyLife, a networking group for Ivy League alums that (among other things) holds weekly breakfasts on Wednesdays in New York City. "I find I'm fresher and more creative in the morning. I'm more open to being inspired by stories I hear around the table," he says. "By the end of the day my mind is a little more cluttered." Any veterans of the happy-hour scene can sympathize—and know that cluttered feeling just gets worse after a few gin and tonics.

2. Nurturing Your Relationships

I first realized that families could treat their mornings as something other than a death march out the door when speaking with Kathryn Beaumont Murphy, a corporate tax attorney whose time makeover I featured in *168 Hours*. A first-year associate when I met her, she had a hard time getting home in the evenings early enough to spend much time with her daughter. This was a source of great frustration for her, even though she was with her daughter a lot on weekends. I looked at her time log and noticed that she puttered around for an extended period at night, then got up, went to work, and puttered around there. She got coffee and checked personal e-mail or read headlines before settling in to work. So I suggested she go to bed on time, get up with her daughter, and use the mornings as Mommy-and-me time before starting her commute. She liked this idea. "It would be so easy to do, I wonder why I didn't think of it," she said. She particularly liked the idea of planning what they'd do together in advance, so she could wake up looking forward to it. Over the next few months, they started making breakfast together, cuddling, or reading stories before her daughter's nanny walked in the door. Given that Murphy's office rewarded late hours, not early hours, I doubted anyone would notice if she came in a little later—closer to the time she truly started working.

It was a nice way to start the day, a nice way to give her daughter her best, rather than what was left over. Indeed, the mornings became so appealing that, when I checked in two years later, Murphy reported that her husband had taken over the mornings as *his* special time with their daughter and the son they had in early 2010. "Breakfast is now a *huge* production in our house," Murphy told me. "I think they all love it!"

This idea of using mornings as positive family time really stuck with me as I looked at my own life. While my kids tend to get up later, many small children wake up at the crack of dawn. So if you work outside the home and don't see your kids during the day, why not take advantage of this? You can keep your eyes constantly focused on the clock, as I have a tendency to do, or you can set an alarm to give yourself a fifteen-minute warning, and then just relax. People always pontificate about how important family dinner is, but this is just not a reality in families with young kids who want to eat at 5:30 or 6:00 p.m., especially if one or both parents work later hours. But there's nothing magical about dinner. Indeed, if the research on will-power is to be believed, we're more crabby at dinner than we are at breakfast. Family breakfasts—when treated as relaxed, fun affairs—are a great substitute for the evening meal. So these days, I'm trying to say yes to making pancakes more often. I try to put off paging through the paper and instead talk to my kids about what's going to happen during the day, or anything they happen to be thinking about.

This is what Judi Rosenthal, a New York–based financial planner and founder of the Bloom network of Ameriprise financial advisors, does. Her husband handles primary parenting duties, but "my morning routine includes special time with my daughter, unless I am on the road," she says. "I always prepare her breakfast (bacon is a key ingredient) and set a beautiful place for her at our table. We sit together and chat about whatever. If we have time, we will do some coloring or 'scissoring' with construction paper and glue. Then we make her bed together and I help her to get dressed, singing songs and brushing hair and chatting away. It's about forty-five minutes of the most precious moments I have in a day."

Even if you don't have kids at home, morning time can be great for nurturing your relationship with your spouse, other family members, or your close friends. One of the most disturbing "statistics" I read while researching how people use their time was that dual-income couples could find only 12 minutes a day to talk with each other. If that's all they can find, they're not looking very hard. A week has 168 hours; if you work 50 hours and sleep 56 (8 per night), that still leaves 62 hours for other things. We can probably find more than 84 minutes (12 × 7) in there somewhere. Nonetheless, couples often feel like ships passing in the night, docking in the same port only when they both land on the couch in front of the TV at day's end.

But some couples manage to get plenty of quality time. By 9:00 a.m. each weekday, Obie McKenzie, managing director in BlackRock's Global Client Group, and his wife have already spent close to 84 minutes chatting to each other, because they drive into New York City from their home in Englewood, New

Jersey, together. This turns what could be an irritating rush-hour trip into a daily date. "It keeps us connected all day long," says McKenzie. They talk through various household details (like repairs after a recent pipe-bursting fiasco), their finances, and life.

Or, as one poster wrote on my blog, describing his ideal morning, there is always "sex at dawn." Not a bad way to fill the time before breakfast, if you think about it.

3. Nurturing Yourself

Most of the executives James Citrin surveyed about their morning routines exercised in some way in the morning. Frits van Paasschen, then president and CEO of the Coors Brewing Company, aimed to be running by 5:50 a.m. and home by 6:30. Ursula Burns, then senior vice president (now CEO) of Xerox, scheduled an hour of personal training starting at 6:00 a.m. two times per week. Steve Murphy, then CEO of Rodale, blocked out ninety minutes for yoga three days a week.

These are incredibly busy people. If they make time to exercise, it must be important, and if they do it in the morning, there's probably a reason. Indeed, some research has suggested that morning exercise has more beneficial effects than exercising at other times. One study, from Appalachian State University, found that people who work out first thing in the morning doze off faster and have less disrupted sleep than those who exercise at other times. One possible explanation is that the body releases stress hormones when you wake up, and working out in the morning counteracts those hormones. Working out later in the day gives the stress hormones more time to take effect. Another study found that early (prebreakfast) vigorous exercise counteracts the blood glucose effects of a high-fat diet, though other research has found better performance after a light breakfast. Regardless, several studies have found a less medically complex reason that morning exercise is more effective: people who work out in the mornings are more likely to stick with it, probably for the same willpower and logistical reasons that we talked about earlier. A one-time run does little for you. A lifetime commitment to run five times per week, on the other hand, will transform your health.

I quite like running already, but in the summer of 2011, I decided to see if running at dawn made me like it more. The answer? Yes. After we moved from Manhattan to the more bucolic wilds of suburban Pennsylvania in June, I began running in the early mornings on the days when my husband was home. I'd lay out my exercise clothes down to the ponytail holder and set my alarm for 6:20. I could be out the door by 6:30, and I'd spend the next forty-five minutes running on some nature trails by our new home. The thick green leaves provided shade, even during days that would eventually rise to one hundred degrees—important, since I was pregnant at the time and didn't want to overheat. I watched earthworms crawl along the pavement, and I startled deer waiting there in the woods. One particularly glorious morning I saw a rainbow, just as I was turning toward home. Running the same routes many mornings, I started to see progress, like being able to run up a switchback hill without stopping. It was a great time to be alone with my thoughts, to think about the book I was trying to finish at the time, and to ponder my hopes for the little girl merrily kicking inside me as she came along for the ride.

Perhaps recognizing the mood-boosting effects of early-morning exercise, plenty of gyms have classes catering to the morning crowd. Julie Delkamiller, an assistant professor of special education, deaf education, and sign language interpreting at the University of Nebraska Omaha, does a jazzercise class at 5:30 a.m. four to five days per week. "The class is about ten minutes from home and with superlight traffic, it is really easy to get there," she says. "I love the community of other women, who help with accountability, and the instructors are so motivating. It's funny, but it is almost a meditative time for me as well. Also, honestly, the class is smaller and I like having more space." She gets home by 6:35 a.m. "Everyone else is sleeping so I don't feel like I've missed out on anything 'important' and yet I am taking care of myself, which has an amazing impact on my productivity throughout the day."

If the prospect of improved productivity isn't enough to get you out of bed, there is always the precommitment strategy—particularly, paying a trainer to meet you and make sure you exercise. When he was in business school at the University of Pennsylvania and trying to buff up for his wedding, David Adelman had the reigning Mr. Baltimore work him out at the Philly Sports Club several mornings per week. He was used to the early-morning workout routine; he and his wife got together after bonding in an excruciatingly tough 6:00 a.m. sweatfest called Barry's Bootcamp in Los Angeles when they were both working at Bain & Company. "We were just friends at the time, but taking that abuse together led us to start dating," he says. After meeting Mr. Baltimore three to four times a week at 7:00 a.m. for several months, Adelman cut quite a dashing figure for his beach wedding. Now, even as he runs Reel Tributes, a personal history documentary company, and has more flexibility, he still likes to work out first thing in the morning. "I like getting it over with," he says. If you exercise later in the day, you may spend time dreading it. If you exercise before most people are eating breakfast, you don't have to think about it long.

Of course, exercise isn't the only thing you can do to nurture yourself. Spiritual practices—praying, devotions, studying scripture, or meditating—are all popular, too. Christine Galib, who used to work in Morgan Stanley's private wealth management practice and who's now a Teach for America corps member working at Boys' Latin school in inner-city Philadelphia, wakes at 5:00 a.m. on weekdays. She does a few biceps curls and plank poses, takes a few minutes to review her tasks for the day, then reads a Bible verse and reflects on it for a few minutes before fetching her breakfast. "Anything I did on Wall Street did not prepare me to teach classes of twenty-five to thirty boys," she says. This ritual "makes my days more manageable."

Wendy Kay, whose work has involved turning around several plasma collection centers (including bringing one that had been shut down back into FDA compliance), says that "my morning ritual of spiritual connection and meditation has been the key to my professional success in my adult life." Through her years working in the pharmaceutical industry, she would wake up two hours before she had to leave the house, and she'd spend a big chunk of this time talking with God, expressing gratitude, asking for guidance, and being open to inspiration. Then she would write down ideas. "When I arrived at work, my vision was always clear, the goals were always clear, and I was able to convey them to my staff and assistants in a clear plan of action," she says.

Manisha Thakor, founder and CEO of MoneyZen Wealth Management, sings the praises of Transcendental Meditation. This consists of two twenty-minute meditation sessions every day. During these sessions, she focuses on breathing and repeating a mantra in her head. She does the first session before breakfast and the second as she's transitioning back to home life in the evening. She began the practice when she shifted from executive to entrepreneur. "The demands were so different, I felt like my work was in my head 24/7/365 and my mind was just never quiet enough for me to create at the level I wanted to." She signed up for training with her husband and has "found it to be one of the most life-enhancing practices I've ever experienced. I think more clearly. Creative ideas 'pop' into my head with more frequency. I am able to look at my day's to-do list with a much calmer and more strategic eye." As a result, it's "made this triple-type-A-driven work junkie a lot more fun to be around."

HOW TO MAKE OVER
YOUR MORNINGS

From studying people's morning habits, I've learned that getting the most out of this time involves a five-step process.

1. Track Your Time

Part of spending your time better is knowing exactly how you're spending it now. If you've ever tried to lose weight, you know that nutritionists tell you to keep a food journal because it keeps you from eating mindlessly. It's the same thing with time. Write down what you're doing as often as you can and in as much detail as you think will be helpful. There's a spread-sheet you can download from http://lauravanderkam.com /books/168-hours/manage-your-time/ or you can just use a little notebook or Word document on your computer.

While you may be thinking specifically about your morn-ings, try tracking a whole week (168 hours). The reason to do this is that the solution to morning dilemmas often lies at other times of the day. You may be too tired in the mornings because you're staying up late. But if you look at how you're spending your nights, you'll notice that you're not doing anything urgent or particularly enjoyable. Jon Stewart's show can be recorded and watched later—possibly while you're on the treadmill at 6:30 a.m. Most of your colleagues wouldn't expect an immediate response to any e-mails sent between 11:00 p.m. and 8:00 a.m. anyway, so why bother checking your in-box? If you're spending time tidying the house, keep in mind that it will just get dirty again the next day, but you'll never get that time back. If you can't sleep in a mess, try just cleaning your bedroom, and closing the doors to the rest of your home.

As for the mornings themselves, you can be spending them in a very organized fashion and still not be spending them in a way that aligns with your values. Track them carefully and question your assumptions. What absolutely has to happen, and what does not? You may believe that "a good mother makes her children's lunches" but I bet you could find several women you believe are incredible mothers who give their kids lunch money. You may believe that "a man who wants to keep his job gets in to the office before his boss" because this is what your father believed, but your boss may be disappointed that he doesn't get the place to himself for an hour first! Does your personal care seem overly fussy? Are your kids demanding that you do things that they are plenty old enough to do on their own? This has been an issue in my house, and part of making over my mornings has been investing time in teaching my children to be more self-reliant. Time not spent chasing down backpacks is time you could spend talking with the kid herself. If you decide that making lunches or being the first person in to your office is a top priority, then do it, but understand that this is a choice and not something you "have" to do.

2. Picture the Perfect Morning

After you know how you're spending your time, ask yourself what a great morning would look like for you. For me, it would start with a run (or, perhaps, sex at dawn per my reader's suggestion) followed by a hearty family breakfast with good coffee, then, after getting people out the door, focused work on a long-term project like a book, plus writing on my personal blog. Here are some other ideas for potential morning habits:

painting, sketching, photography (if it's light out), scrapbooking, crafts, writing poetry, practicing a musical instrument (if you live by yourself), reading through a religious text verse by verse, yoga, Zumba class, walking, training for a half marathon, biking, swimming, working out with a trainer, weight lifting, prayer, reading through a book of devotions, looking through your photo albums or contact list and praying for people by name, meditation, making a gratitude list, writing your own blog, writing "Morning Pages" (per Julia Cameron's *The Artist's Way*), writing one thousand words in a novel, writing in a journal, writing thank-you letters, reading articles in professional journals, attending a regular networking breakfast, having family breakfast, making pancakes or baking with your kids, reading together for a family book club, reading kids' stories, reading through all the plays of Shakespeare, reading through the best novels of the twentieth century, listening to challenging music like Wagner's Ring Cycle, playing with your kids, doing art projects with your kids, gardening, exercising with your spouse, trying a new recipe every morning, strategic career thinking, planning long-term employee career development, brainstorming new business lines or sales prospects, coming up with new projects or initiatives, studying, taking a self-paced online class

3. Think Through the Logistics

How could this vision mesh with the life you have? How long will your ritual take? Don't assume you have to add it on top of the hours you already spend getting ready or that you'll have to get in to work earlier. The good thing about filling the morning hours with important activities is that you'll crowd out things that are more time intensive than they need to be. Give yourself fifteen minutes for a shower and you'll take fifteen minutes; give yourself five and you'll be out in five. Unless, of course, your ideal morning ritual is a contemplative shower, in which case stay in there as long as you can. Map out a morning schedule. What would have to happen to make this schedule work? What time would you have to get up and (most important) what time do you need to go to bed in order to get enough sleep? Can you get to bed by that time? People who are used to staying up late may find that counting back eight hours from the time they'd like to get up suggests an improbably early bedtime, but there are plenty of ways to wind down so you won't toss and turn. Stop watching TV or checking e-mail an hour before bed (there's some evidence that screen light can interfere with sleep patterns). Make sure your room is dark and a little cool. Wear earplugs if others are still up and about. Try taking some deep breaths, meditating, praying, writing in a journal, or reading something relaxing to calm yourself down.

As for the mornings themselves, do you need to trade off child-care duties with your partner or hire a sitter some mornings or get your kids to school or day care earlier? Do you need exercise equipment? Can you work in a home office and buy back your commute time? Can you carpool with a family member or friend?

What would make your ritual easier? Do you need to set your easel next to your bed? Can you find a more cheerful alarm clock, or one you can't turn off so easily?

Come up with a plan and assemble what you need, but whatever you do, don't label this vision as impossible. It's easy to believe our own excuses, particularly if they're good ones. For instance, maybe you're telling yourself that you can't use your mornings to exercise because you're a single parent of small children (or a single parent during the week, a challenge I sometimes face). But, for a moment, forget financial constraints. Pretend you had all the money in the world and list as many options as you can think of, which you'll soon see involve varying costs and degrees of difficulty. You could, for instance, hire a live-in nanny or au pair or bribe a relative to move in with you. You could get a housemate—perhaps another single parent you would in turn cover for when she wanted to work out. You could hire an early-morning sitter on the mornings you planned to exercise, or ask a relative or friend to come over on those mornings. You could find a day-care or before-school program with early hours, or a gym with child care. You could buy a treadmill (new or used) and put it in your basement in front of a television and run before the kids get up. You could buy a double jogging stroller and take the kids with you. Looking at the list, the used treadmill seems most cost-efficient and least logistically difficult to me, but maybe you'll decide one of the other options sounds appealing instead.

4. Build the Habit

This is the most important step. Turning a desire into a ritual requires a lot of initial willpower, and not just for the first few days. The first few days you have enough motivation to move mountains at 5:30 a.m., but then, around day thirteen, you're wavering, and your bed will start to seem pretty enticing. What should you do?

One answer is to start slowly. Go to bed fifteen minutes earlier and wake up fifteen minutes earlier for a few days until this new schedule seems doable.

Monitor your energy. Building a new habit takes effort, so you want to take care of yourself while you're trying. Eat right and eat enough, take breaks during your workday, and surround yourself with supportive people who want to see you succeed.

Choose one new habit at a time to introduce. If you want to run, pray, and write in a journal each morning, choose one of these and put all your energy into making that activity a habit before you try something else.

Chart your progress. Habits take several weeks to establish, so keep track of how you're doing for at least thirty days. In his writings, Ben Franklin described how he scored himself for practicing various virtues (temperance, modesty, and the like). It's an idea Gretchen Rubin ran with in *The Happiness Project*, noting victories on her Resolutions Chart when she made progress toward her goals. Once skipping a day feels like you forgot something—like forgetting to brush your teeth—you'll know you've got a habit and can take your ritual up a notch.

Also, feel free to use bribery at first. Eventually daily exercise will produce its own motivation as you start to look better and have more energy. But until then, external motivations, like promising yourself tickets to a concert or a massage, can keep you moving forward. And keep in mind that your morning rituals shouldn't be of the self-flagellation variety. Choose things you actually enjoy. Shawn Achor, author of *The Happiness Advantage* and a self-proclaimed night owl, trained himself to become a morning person by creating rituals that make him excited to get out of bed. He starts the day by writing down things he's thankful for. "The reason we stay in bed in the morning is because our brains get fatigued by thinking about all the things we have to do that day. We're thinking about tasks rather than things that are making us happy," he says. But the reverse of that is also true. "If you're thinking about things you're looking forward to, that makes it easy to get out of bed. What your brain focuses on becomes your reality."

In addition to listing things he's grateful for, Achor also uses a few of his morning minutes to write a quick appreciation e-mail to a friend or family member, or even a thank-you note to a high school English teacher. This puts him in a loving, connected frame of mind. "It's usually my favorite part of the whole day," he says. With that done before breakfast, it's not hard to face the morning.

5. Tune Up as Necessary

Life changes. Rituals can change, too. My morning ritual of running with the sunrise disappeared with summer as I finally became too pregnant to do so comfortably. After Ruth's birth, I chose to run in the early afternoons again, when it was light out and warmer, and since I never knew exactly what time she would wake up in the morning wanting to eat. I've started working, instead, on eating a relaxed breakfast with my kids and maybe reading them a few stories before using my morning burst of productivity to tackle one of my longer writing projects. But after my baby grows up a little, I look forward to returning to those morning runs, when the fresh morning air makes you feel like every day is full of possibility.

Because that is ultimately the amazing thing about mornings—they always feel like a new chance to do things right. A win scored then creates a "cascade of success," says Achor. "Once your brain records a victory it's more likely to take the next step and the next step." Believing that your actions matter is how the human mind learns optimism or, to use a better word, hope.

The most successful people know that the hopeful hours before most people eat breakfast are far too precious to be blown on semiconscious activities. You can do a lot with those hours. Randeep Rekhi of Colorado works full-time in a financial services firm. But by the time he shows up at his office at 8:00 a.m., he's already worked out and managed a side business, the website of his family's wine store, WineDelight.com. He wakes at 5:00 a.m. and heads straight to his apartment gym to exercise until 6:00 or so. Then he spends the next ninety minutes on his computer, checking the site's incoming traffic and answering customer e-mails. "After work usually quickly books up with networking events, happy hours, et cetera, so the morning is really the only guaranteed time I can have to myself without sacrificing other opportunities," he says. I cringe thinking about getting up at 5:00 a.m., but the reality is I'm rarely doing much of consequence after 10:00 p.m. Whenever I'm tempted to say I don't have time for something, I remind myself that if I wanted to get up early, I could. These hours are available to all of us if we choose to use them.

So how would you like to use your mornings? As with any other important question, this one repays careful thinking, spending time figuring out what is truly meaningful to you. But once you decide, small rituals can accomplish great things. A habit, Anthony Trollope once said, "has the force of the water drop that hollows the stone. A small daily task, if it be really daily, will beat the labors of a spasmodic Hercules."

When you make over your mornings, you can make over your life. That is what the most successful people know.

WHAT THE MOST

DO ON THE WEEKEND

THE PARADOX OF WEEKENDS

Mike Huckabee is a busy man. The ordained Baptist minister and former governor of Arkansas ran for president in 2008, but when that didn't work out he became a Republican Party influencer, raising money and campaigning for candidates who share his views. He's just published his tenth book, he hosts a three-hour daily radio show during the week, and on Thursdays he travels to New York City from his home in Florida in preparation to tape his Fox News show, *Huckabee.* You don't have to agree with his politics to see that this is an exhausting schedule, particularly because he records his television show on Saturdays, guaranteeing him a six-day workweek. What makes it all possible?

Sundays. "That's pretty much my day to try to rest and have what I call some 'Mike time,'" Huckabee says. "It's almost like running a marathon. You think, I know the finish line is out there, and you start visioning the finish line. Many days of the week I start visioning Sunday as the day I can kind of catch my breath. I'm not on someone else's schedule and I don't have to turn on a mic at a certain time." From the time his plane lands at 7:45 p.m. on Saturday to the time he's recording a short

Huckabee Report commentary later Sunday evening, "it's my time just to mentally recharge."

But what Huckabee describes as a "leisurely" day is far from slothful. "I'm a structured and orderly person," he says, and because his downtime is so limited, he has to be careful about how he spends it. "I almost never just sit and watch television," he says. Instead, Huckabee has a plan. He gets up around 6:00 a.m. on Sunday morning and works out on the recumbent bike and elliptical machine while reading several newspapers (physical papers on the bike; electronic papers on the elliptical). He and his wife, Janet, attend the 10:45 a.m. service at Destiny Worship Center, where the music is contemporary, the preacher is "fantastic," and "if you want to wear shorts and dress in beach style, that's perfectly fine." After lunch, Huckabee does in fact hit the beach. "The weather almost compels me to be outdoors," he says, and he usually spends the afternoon "sitting on the beach and listening to nothing but the seagulls and the waves crash against the shore." Come dinnertime, the Huckabees often have friends over, with Huckabee cooking—a hobby he confesses to enjoying. Mostly it's steaks or fish on the grill, or a tenderloin or ribs in the electric smoker. "It's really kind of a good time," he says. Indeed, if weekdays feature the things he has to do, Sundays feature "all the things that I would want to do."

Having recharged the batteries, Huckabee hits Monday relaxed, refreshed, and ready to take on the world. As he ponders how to describe his philosophy toward weekends, he offers two seemingly contradictory ideas. First, you have to commit to taking time off—to keep a Sabbath of sorts, and carve out space for rest in a frenetic world. But second, you have to realize that this rest time is too precious to be totally leisurely about leisure. "Don't enter into it with such a lack of structure that you don't do anything because you spend all day thinking about what you want to do," Huckabee advises. "If you know you want to read a book, then get the book out and have it set aside and make plans to read it. Say it's going to be at one. When that starts, get on it. Don't wait until that afternoon, then think—could I read? Or listen to some music? Or take a walk? Then you'll sit about wasting an hour of what little time you have figuring out what to do with the rest of it." To make the most of your weekends, "you tell yourself, 'Look, what would make me really, really enjoy this day and kind of get me out of the normal routine and give me pleasure?'" Then say, "This is what I'm going to do," and come that time, be disciplined about that commitment, telling yourself, "This is my appointment, just as if it's a doctor's appointment or an appointment to go to work."

This is the paradox of weekends: "You have to set an appointment to go off the grid as surely as to go on it."

The Quest for Rejuvenation

Having seen hundreds of time logs over the years, I think Huckabee is on to something. If you have a demanding job— the kind that requires turning off your cell phone at midnight because otherwise it will keep ringing, where you leave on a plane Monday and come home Thursday just hoping you haven't crossed too many time zones, where whole afternoons disappear into e-mail firefights—then you know weekends are what stand between you and a smoldering burnout. Success in a competitive world requires hitting Monday refreshed and ready to go. The only way to do that is to create weekends that rejuvenate you rather than exhaust or disappoint you.

Yet many of us have trouble using our weekends well. Even people who are mindful of how they spend their weekdays find weekends slipping through their fingers. These days disappear into chores, errands, inefficient e-mail checking, unconsciously chosen television marathons, or a death march of children's activities that suck the energy out of chauffeuring adults. Learning to create restorative weekends requires thinking about weekends differently than we're used to and, in many cases, than at first we think we want to. We need to be strategic with these hours.

How many hours? Just as using weekends well requires embracing a paradox, weekends themselves are both expansive but not as infinite as they seem. While some folks like Huckabee have six-day workweeks, most of us think of the weekend as Saturday and Sunday—and, in fact, the weekend is a little longer than that. There are sixty hours between the moment you crack open a beer at 6:00 p.m. Friday and the time the alarm goes off at 6:00 a.m. Monday. Sixty hours is a decently high percentage of a 168-hour week. Even if you're asleep for twenty-four of those hours, that still leaves thirty-six hours for waking rejuvenation. That's the equivalent of a full-time job—and this is a helpful mind-set to have. You would not take a thirty-six-hour-per-week job without asking what you intended to do with it and what you expect the outcome to be.

On the other hand, while these sixty-hour blocks are lengthy, they don't come in an unlimited supply. You have fewer than one thousand Saturdays with each child in your care before he or she is grown up. Even more fleeting? Those perfect weekends that so encapsulate their season that they become entwined with your memory of that time. Here in the Northeast, each autumn there are only about three weekends when the trees flash their full, glorious color before winter winds scuttle the leaves away. If you live to be eighty, that's only 240 weekends when the maples are blazing scarlet—and you likely don't remember at least a tenth of those. These numbered weekends pass whether we think about how to spend them or not. While it seems like there will always be another weekend—another weekend when we will be less tired, less stressed, more adventurous—time is far from infinite.

Successful people know that weekends deserve even more care than you bestow on your working days. Every week, you are granted another chance to spend your time becoming happier, more creative, and whole. How do you achieve this rejuvenation? How do you arrange your weekend hours to create, over time, a full life? That is the subject of this part of the book, and the answer starts by taking a slightly different approach to a common question.

"What Are We Doing This Weekend?"

If your household is like mine, the question of what you're doing this weekend often doesn't get asked until Friday sneaks up on you, and sometimes not until everyone rolls out of bed on Saturday morning. If you've spent the week battling traffic or collecting frequent-flier miles, you may think you want the answer to be "nothing."

It holds a certain appeal. We picture lazy days spent lounging around in pajamas, or as John Keats wrote in his poem "Ode on Indolence," lying "cool-bedded in the flowery grass." It's an alluring image, as long as you remember that Keats didn't have children, and he lived long before television and the Internet. In our distracted world, we're constantly battling electronic temptations that threaten to take over our available time. While "nothing" in Keats's day meant watching the clouds float by, "nothing" now means weekend hours parked on the sofa watching television we didn't mean to watch, surfing websites we didn't plan to surf, and checking e-mail in an inefficient manner. One recent study from UCLA's Center on the Everyday Lives of Families found that adults in dual-income, middle-class Los Angeles homes spent fewer than fifteen minutes of leisure time per week out in their backyards. They had leisure time—far more than fifteen minutes per week. They had great weather and lovely porch furniture. They just didn't use it. In a world of constant connectivity, even loafing time must be consciously chosen, because time will be filled with something, whether it's consciously chosen or not—and not choosing means that the something that fills our hours will be less fulfilling than the something our remembering selves will likely wish we'd elected to do.

This reality is more pronounced if you have little ones at home. In my house, doing "nothing" still means caring for three children under the age of six. Stay-at-home parents certainly don't think of themselves as doing nothing during the week, and one reason they make playdates and go to art classes is that staying home with bickering small children is more exhausting than distracting them with something else, something chosen—ideally something that the parent enjoys, too.

What all this means is that Huckabee's appeal to structure is worth a thought. I find it leads to two decisions that together create weekends that leave you rejuvenated and ready to go: choosing labors of a different sort and embracing anticipation.

Choose Labors of a Different Sort

Yes, your weekends should be different from your workdays. Yes, you need a kind of rest. Ted Devine, CEO of Insureon and former CEO of Aon Re, who coaches youth hockey on his weekends, draws an analogy from that sport. "You have to go as hard as you can for a minute and a half on the ice, then get off the ice and rest your legs—and if you don't do that, you won't go out the next shift and play nearly as well," he says. But I think (given that Devine is coaching hockey on his weekends, and not sitting on a bench!) the best sports analogy is that of "active rest" or cross-training.

I discovered the benefits of cross-training in the athletic side of my life when I signed up to run the Big Sur Marathon in April 2010. I'd had a baby in late September 2009, and while I'd run through the pregnancy, my volume of miles in the last trimester and first postpartum weeks was—not surprisingly— lower than most training plans recommend. I knew that ramping up mileage too quickly could cause the shin splints, busted knees, and cases of Achilles tendonitis that plague would-be marathoners. Fortunately, I came across a training book called *Run Less, Run Faster* by Bill Pierce, Scott Murr, and Ray Moss. Their plan advocates skipping "junk miles" and biking, swimming, or doing other sports instead. "If running is your only mode of exercise, the same muscles are always stressed in the same way, increasing the likelihood of injury," the authors write. "Cross-training allows for a tremendous volume of central circulatory training without overusing a particular muscle group. . . . [Cross-training] helps you avoid boredom and burnout and keeps up your zest for training." I never ran more than thirty-five miles per week, but I finished the marathon in good enough shape to hike with my family the next day. Cross-training was better for my running than sitting on the couch or more running. Likewise, other kinds of work—be it exercise, a creative hobby, hands-on parenting, or volunteering—will do more to preserve your zest for Monday's challenges than complete vegetation or working through the weekend. As Anatole France once wrote, "Man is so made that he can only find relaxation from one kind of labor by taking up another."

This theme—trading one labor for another—pervades the *New York Times* series on famous New Yorkers called "My Sunday Routine." Architect Rafael Viñoly, according to his November 13, 2011, profile, on Sundays plays the piano for several hours. "My pianos are my only big indulgence, but they're a necessity," he said. "When I'm playing the piano is literally the only time I can be completely abstract and disconnected from the regular world and yet be connected—to my music."

Celebrity chef Marcus Samuelsson, according to his profile, on weekends plays soccer in Chinatown with fellow Swedish expats. "It's not so much about the playing as about being with friends with a common background," he told the *Times*. "On the field, anything goes. It's a way to blow off steam and say things you can't say in the kitchen anymore." If Samuelsson doesn't have a game, he runs six miles or so in Central Park. "While I run, I think about food," he said. But needless to say, one likely has different thoughts about food while sweating around airy running paths than one would in a crowded kitchen.

This different approach to thinking is why Dominique Schurman, CEO of the stationery company Papyrus, calls exercise "almost a job requirement. It allows me to kind of release the tension and clear my head. I get a lot of ideas when I'm exercising," she told me. She goes on long runs and swims, and also gardens—a physical activity that she calls "a creative outlet. I just like to work on what goes well together." As she moves her pots around, she studies different ways to combine color and texture, not unlike what she asks her card designers to do during the week. "Since I do that in my job, I kind of enjoy a tactile dimension," she says. "I find that relaxing."

Of course, sometimes the appeal of doing something physical is that you can't ruminate in quite the same way as you would at your workplace. Bill McGowan, a television correspondent who's won two Emmys for his coverage, calls himself a "big woodchopper." He and his wife moved to a somewhat overgrown property on the Hudson River in Westchester, New York, about five years ago and had a few trees taken down. "I like to take these big cylinders—two to three feet wide in diameter—and chop them into firewood," he says. Aside from being very good exercise, "I find it this incredibly

Zen experience," he says, as he tackles a challenge that's very different from the nine-to-five.

Embrace Anticipation

While playing the piano, meeting friends for a soccer game, and chopping wood could be spontaneous activities, for the busiest people, Huckabee is right that you have to make an appointment to go off the grid as surely as to go on it. If you have a three-year-old, for instance, and you wish to chop wood, you need to make sure someone else is dealing with the child so he doesn't decide to "help" you. That requires thinking through your plan for the day and communicating it with your partner or someone else who might watch the child, or even just sticking him in front of the TV so he doesn't stick himself anywhere near the ax. If you're meeting friends to play soccer, you all need to know where and when to meet—even if it's a long tradition. Joan Blades, cofounder of MoveOn.org and Moms Rising.org, plays soccer every Sunday. "This is the same game [my husband] Wes and I met at thirty years ago," she told me. "Some of the players are in their sixties and others are kids. It is a fun game!" But, of course, it's also a game happening at a certain time and place. Playing the piano for hours means making a commitment not to call an equally busy client or look over endless project plans at that time. Eating dinner somewhere lovely often requires a reservation. Any parent knows it's near impossible to get a Saturday-night sitter on Saturday. Going to worship services often requires getting up and getting dressed at a certain time. Failing to think through what you wish to do on the weekend may make you succumb to the "I'm tired" excuse that keeps you locked in the house and not doing anything meaningful within it—even though we draw energy from meaningful things.

And so we come to the insight on weekends that I find people resist: a good weekend needs a plan. Not a minute-by-minute plan, not a spreadsheet full of details, but just a few fun anchor events sketched in ahead of time. Indeed, some research is finding that skipping the planning stage means cutting yourself off from the major mechanism via which weekends can deliver joy.

Harvard psychologist Daniel Gilbert talks about this phenomenon in his 2006 book, *Stumbling on Happiness*. "The greatest achievement of the human brain is its ability to imagine objects and episodes that do not exist in the realm of the real," he writes. "The frontal lobe—the last part of the human brain to evolve, the slowest to mature, and the first to deteriorate in old age—is a time machine that allows each of us to vacate the present and experience the future before it happens."

This time travel into the future—otherwise known as anticipation—accounts for a big chunk of the happiness gleaned from any event. As you look forward to something good that is about to happen, you experience some of the same joy you would in the moment. The major difference is that the joy can last much longer. Consider that ritual of opening presents on Christmas morning. The reality of it seldom takes more than an hour, but the anticipation of seeing the presents under the tree can stretch out the joy for weeks. One study by several Dutch researchers, published in the journal *Applied Research in Quality of Life* in 2010, found that vacationers were happier than people who didn't take holiday trips. That finding is hardly surprising. What is surprising is the timing of the happiness boost. It didn't come after the vacations, with tourists bathing in their post-trip glow. It didn't even come through that strongly during the trips, as the joy of travel mingled with the stress of travel: jet lag, stomach woes, and train conductors giving garbled instructions over the loudspeaker. The happiness boost came before the trips, stretching out for as much as two months beforehand as the holidaygoers imagined their excursions. A vision of little umbrella-sporting drinks can create the happiness rush of a minivacation even in the midst of a rainy commute.

On some level, people instinctively know this. In one study that Gilbert writes about, people were told they'd won a free dinner at a fancy French restaurant. When asked when they'd like to schedule the dinner, most people didn't want to head over right then. They wanted to wait, on average, over a week—to savor the anticipation of their fine fare and to optimize their pleasure. The experiencing self seldom encounters pure bliss, but the anticipating self never has to go to the bathroom in the middle of a favorite band's concert and is never cold from too much air-conditioning in that theater showing the sequel to a favorite flick. Planning a few anchor events for a weekend guarantees you pleasure because—even if all goes wrong in the moment—you still will have derived some pleasure from the anticipation. I love spontaneity and embrace it when it happens, but I cannot bank my pleasure solely on it. If you wait until Saturday morning to make your plans for the weekend, you will spend a chunk of your Saturday working on such plans, rather than anticipating your fun. Hitting the weekend without a plan means you may not get to do what you want. You'll use up energy in negotiations with other family members. You'll start late and the museum will close when you've been there only an hour. Your favorite restaurant will be booked up—and even if, miraculously, you score a table, think of how much more you would have enjoyed the last few days knowing that you'd be eating those seared scallops on Saturday night!

I'm a planner, so this seems intuitive to me. Yet whenever I suggest planning weekends at least a day or two in advance, I get grumbles. First, a great many people simply dislike the idea of planning their leisure time. I think this (mostly) stems from a misunderstanding of what I'm talking about. As one person commented on my blog, "Not everybody wants to fill in every hour every day of the year." I don't want to fill every hour, either. Life would be dreary if you kept your work schedule—planned in fifteen-minute increments—on weekends, too. But there is a wide gap between planning every minute and planning nothing. This is a false choice. I find that three to five anchor events, spread over the sixty hours between that Friday beer and Monday alarm clock, should give you a nice balance. Three things taking three hours apiece is nine hours of your thirty-six waking ones. That leaves a lot of time for sitting and nursing a scotch, if you don't have three small children, or watching *The Backyardigans*, if you do.

Second, I think people have a visceral reaction to the word "plan" that makes them think of things they *don't want* to do. I'm suggesting planning things that you *want* to do. Taking your car to get repaired isn't an anchor event unless you collect antique cars and have a group of friends who meet every

Saturday morning to tinker with them. You seldom hear from a Phillies fan, "Man, I have to go to the game this weekend—I wish I were doing nothing instead." That is the sort of thing that's an anchor event. Humans don't do well with suffering long term. As one reader told me, "Weekends are precious and ought to be cultivated with an eye toward enjoyment." When you plan enjoyable things ahead of time, you magnify the pleasure.

HOW TO PLAN A WEEKEND

Your List of 100 Dreams

With that in mind, we come to the more specific question of figuring out what to do this weekend. Perhaps the best way to frame this question is to ask, "What do you want to do more of with your time?"

We may have vague ideas, but it's more effective to have a really good list. In my first time management book, *168 Hours*, I suggested people create something called a List of 100 Dreams. This exercise, shared with me by career coach Caroline Ceniza-Levine, prompts you to brainstorm anything you might want to do or have in life. When I have people try this in workshops, inevitably the first dreams people suggest are along the lines of "go see the pyramids in Egypt." By Dream 100, however, you'll be coming up with more everyday founts of joy, which tend to make excellent weekend anchor events. You won't have a private dinner catered by Alain Ducasse at the Louvre this weekend. You could, however, let the munchkins run wild on the kiddie rides at the county fair while Mom and Dad indulge in some comically large milk shakes. Keep going until you have a good long list of these doable dreams. You could also think of these as a bucket list focused on activities within a two-hour radius from your house.

SOME ENTRIES IN MY MOST RECENT LIST OF 100 DREAMS

- Bike the Lehigh Gorge State Park trail near Jim Thorpe, Pennsylvania
- Eat lobster on the waterfront near Cape May, New Jersey
- Go for a long run (or a bike ride with the kids in tow) at the Valley Forge battlefield
- Enjoy the Friday evening hours at the Philadelphia Museum of Art
- Eat dinner anywhere with a Zagat rating of 23 or above
- Go on a forty-minute trail run right by my house
- Take in a good choral concert
- Pick apples or strawberries with the kids
- Get my husband to grill a steak for me
- Have friends over for summer dinners and a dip in the pool
- Visit Longwood Gardens during spring weekends when the trees look like cotton candy

What's on your List of 100 Dreams?

Set Anchors

Start working on your list, and ask your significant other, kids, or anyone you spend weekends with to come up with a list, too. Keep adding to it. If you're stumped, you might hit the library and check out a book on tourist highlights for your city. Also, feel free to modify the list as needed. Once you try a particular activity, you may decide that you've had enough strawberry picking to last a lifetime and need not try that again. But be sure to keep the list somewhere accessible. Because ideally, in consultation with your fellow travelers at some point before the weekend, you can pluck items from your happy list, add new opportunities that come up, and peg them to the major weekend spots:

- Friday night
- Saturday day
- Saturday night
- Sunday day
- Sunday night

This planning meeting can be as fun as you want: one busy woman tells me that she and her husband sit down with beers on Friday to plan out their weekends. It's more about catching up and brainstorming what they'll do (and drinking beer) than a chore.

You can plan as loosely as you like. "Dinner with Joan and Bob along the waterfront" is perfectly fine—you can meet and stroll along, checking out restaurants and picking one that's most enticing. Andrea Wilhelm, a quality assurance specialist at Epic, a health-care software company, moved to Madison, Wisconsin, last year after graduating from college. Madison is often ranked as one of the best U.S. cities for young adults, and she's been trying to take advantage of the city as systematically as possible. "I like having things loosely planned because it gives me the freedom to do lots of different things," she says. She also wants to avoid the feeling that she's wasting her time in the town. "If/when I move on from Madison, I don't want to look back and be, like, 'Man, I wish I went there' or 'I never got around to doing that.'" On Friday nights, she goes to different restaurants or bars with friends. On Saturdays, after mornings devoted to taking online classes and an afternoon volleyball game, she goes to shows and different entertainment centers around the city. "Being an outdoorsy person, Sundays are great for getting friends together for these types of events"—meaning hikes, bike rides, and the like—"because they usually attract smaller crowds."

Even "fun family excursion" can work as a planning entry. Simply knowing that you and the kids will be leaving the house for the afternoon can add order to the day. Laura Overdeck, founder of Bedtime Math and a trustee at New Jersey's Liberty Science Center, does a lot of these excursions with her three kids. "It's different every time, and usually on a whim depending on our collective mood," she says. "Examples of favorites are Liberty Science Center"—of course—"and in fall and spring, if we wake up and the weather's nice, we'll head to the beach just to dig in the sand, or take the kids apple or berry picking, or hang out with Grandma and Grandpa, who luckily live nearby."

Your three to five anchor events can be whatever you like, but research suggests some optimal pairings. Huckabee's weekend features time on the bike, church, and dinner with friends, and it turns out this sort of portfolio maximizes happiness returns. One study of Texas workingwomen, published in *Science* in 2004, charted their experienced happiness through the day. Beyond obviously pleasurable activities like eating, relaxing, and sex—all of which are great to do on weekends—the researchers found that these women were happiest when exercising, engaging in spiritual activities, and socializing. So why not aim for at least one item from these three categories? You can even combine them. Lorie Marrero, founder of the Clutter Diet organizing company, reports, "One of the things I have done with weekends is used the time to catch up with friends doing the 'walk and talk.'" She meets a friend on Sunday mornings at a trail and walks for about an hour and a half. "It's exercise, it's chatting, and it's not a typical 'let's have lunch or coffee' thing," she says. "I don't have to wear makeup and it feels very relaxing."

Here are some other examples of awesome weekends.

WEEKEND #1
- Friday evening: Friends over for game night
- Saturday day: Family beach trip
- Saturday evening: Family dinner at a restaurant near the beach that you've been meaning to try
- Sunday day: Church
- Sunday evening: Leisurely walk around the neighborhood

WEEKEND #2
- Friday evening: Karaoke at a bar with friends
- Saturday day: Volunteer shift at a soup kitchen
- Saturday evening: Concert in the park
- Sunday day: Long run to local farmers' market, then take bus home
- Sunday evening: Yoga class

WEEKEND #3
- Friday evening: Dinner and a movie
- Saturday day: Hike with friends
- Saturday evening: Birthday party
- Sunday day: Meditation session
- Sunday evening: Dinner and dancing at a street fair

WEEKEND #4
- Friday evening: Bike rides and then out for ice cream
- Saturday day: Picnic lunch while watching a soccer game
- Saturday evening: Cookout with the neighbors
- Sunday day: Trip to the zoo
- Sunday evening: Volunteer as a family to help clean a local park

Six Secrets of Successful Weekends

Here are a few more tips to remember as you're making your plans.

1. Dig deep. Just because you haven't done something in years doesn't mean it can't be on your List of 100 Dreams. Maybe there are activities you haven't done since childhood that could become a regular part of your weekends. One reader tells me that she and her husband decided to sign up for piano lessons on Saturday mornings. Now they and their teenage son all have lessons back-to-back. It's easier to nudge a kid to practice when Mom and Dad are doing it, too. Sometimes we get so concerned about scheduling our kids' lives that we forget to schedule our own.

2. Use your mornings. Weekend mornings tend to be wasted time, but they're great for personal pursuits. If you're training for a marathon, it's less disruptive for your family if you get up early to do your four-hour run than if you try to do it in the middle of the day. To get up early, you'll probably have to avoid staying up late the night before, but this is a good idea in general.

3. Create traditions. Happy families often have some special weekend activity that everyone loves but no one has to plan each time. Maybe it's pancakes on Saturday mornings or a family walk to worship services, but whatever it is, make a ritual of it. These habits are what become memories—and comforting rituals boost happiness.

4. Schedule downtime. Jess Lahey, a New Hampshire–based teacher and writer, has official weekend naptime in her house that takes place each afternoon between 1:00 and 3:00. Her kids—who are preteens, not toddlers who actually need to nap— know it's coming, and they save up screen time for it. They play games together, watch a movie, or read. Everyone turns their phones off, and Lahey and her husband close the door to the upstairs, read for a bit, "then dive in for what always proves to be kick-ass sleep. That deep sleep that leaves you a little disoriented when you wake up," she says. "Once I've figured out where I am and what day it is, I leap out of bed recharged and head out to weed the garden or get down to the business of making dinner."

5. Make time to explore. A run, walk, or bike ride can turn into an adventure—with plenty of opportunities for that spontaneity people seem to think planning quashes—if you choose the right neighborhood. Use weekends to stretch your routine a bit.

6. Plan something fun for Sunday nights. This idea may be the most important tip in this book. Even if you love your job, it's easy to feel a bit of trepidation on Sunday about the stresses waiting for you on Monday morning. And if you don't like your job, Sunday trepidation can become a full-on case of the Sunday-night blues as time slides, inexorably, into the next day. You wonder what you're doing with your life. You wonder if any of it is worthwhile.

If you're asking such existential questions, it may be time to shake things up. But in the meantime, or even if you just feel weary when you think of your commute, you can combat the Sunday-night blues by scheduling something fun for Sunday evening. This extends the weekend and keeps you focused on the fun to come, rather than on Monday morning.

Caitlin Andrews, a librarian, calls it a "necessity" to end Sunday night on a high note. Her extended family gets together for dinner almost every Sunday, alternating houses. "The host house cooks the main meal but the others bring something to add—an appetizer, a bottle of wine, a side dish, or dessert. It's a little stressful when I have to cook and clean for people coming over," she reports, "but I don't spend too much time on it and my husband helps. Plus, we always end up with leftovers for the rest of the week when we cook. It's just a couple of hours—everyone comes over about five thirty and we're home by eight or nine." That's plenty of time to plan and decompress before bed, and she looks forward to this tradition all weekend. "It takes my mind off any Sunday-night blues that might be coming on."

Aliza Rosen, a reality TV producer who's dreamed up series like *Farm Kings* and *Curvy Girls*, does yoga at 6:00 p.m. on Sundays. "It's a great way for me to sweat out the toxins of the week and center myself for Monday," she says. "I reset myself." She admits that, for her, the yoga is not particularly spiritual. "I'm making a mental list," she says. But it gives her something to anticipate as she's sliding toward each Monday firefight. That may be the same thing that Ina Garten, the chef otherwise known as the Barefoot Contessa, was thinking when she created her 6:00 p.m. Sunday ritual of getting a massage. According to the July 1, 2012, "My Sunday Routine" *New York Times* profile of Garten, this twenty-seven-year tradition stemmed from a 1985 realization that "I was working really hard, and one day I told myself, 'I'm not having enough fun.' So I did two things: I got myself a red Mustang convertible and started having massages. I don't have the Mustang anymore, but I still have the same masseuse!"

One equally great way to end the weekend is to volunteer. Nothing will take your mind off any problems associated with your decent-paying and steady job like serving people who aren't so fortunate. Savvy volunteer coordinators know that it's easier for most people to make Sunday-night volunteering a part of their lives than other times. Jacob Lee runs the Orange County, California, chapter of the Fellowship of Orthodox Christians United to Serve (FOCUS). Every Sunday night, his volunteers serve a meal, restaurant style, to homeless families living in an area motel. Sunday is "generally kind of a dead night," Lee says. "On Saturday night people have things to do. On Sunday . . . ?" Miraculously, everyone is free. So you get a much more diverse group of volunteers than the retirees and homemakers who might volunteer during the week. After the volunteers serve the meal, as the evening starts to wind down, everyone sits together, telling their life stories and "learning about why people end up where they end up," says Lee. It's a way to connect with humanity before everyone goes their separate ways for the week.

MINIMIZE THE HAVE-TO-DOS

Even if you plan three to five anchor events for your weekends, you'll still see that this leaves plenty of open time. So what should you do with it? You can relax, of course, or be spontaneous. You can play with your kids or lie in the grass. But what about those have-to-dos? What about chores, errands, and playing catch-up on busywork for your paid job? Successful people know that the best weekends feature activities you love and a minimal amount of anything else. In this section, we look at how to handle three common causes of weekend stress: chores, children's activities, and work that follows you home.

Compress the Chores

If you put in long hours at the office or travel much of the week, weekends may seem like a great time to get caught up on chores. But I'm not so sure they are, or that the accomplishment of chores should be too central to your weekends.

The big reason is that many chores expand to fill the available time. Take the procurement of groceries and household supplies. Some items, like diapers, are hard to substitute. Others less so. If you go to the grocery store when the cupboard starts looking bare, you'll buy your usual breakfast cereals. If you don't go? You might eat through that Costco-size bag of English muffins you're storing in the freezer. Chances are you won't starve. Obviously, grocery shopping has to happen at some point, but a late-weekday-evening visit can make for an efficient trip. Or, if you live near a big city, you can order groceries online during a boring conference call. Then it's done without sacrificing weekend time.

A similar thing happens with laundry. We do it most weeks, but we have enough clothes to go longer between loads and we could rewear more items than we do. As for house cleaning, whole treatises have been written on the elasticity of standards. You can clean the toilets once a week and pick up the kitchen when it's awful, or you can dust every bit of your millwork daily. A lot of this comes down more to preference (or budget to pay a housekeeper) than anything else. If you use weekdays for chores, rather than weekends, you may just spend less time on chores—because you have less time. The time you don't spend on chores can be freed up for more meaningful things. Choices are seldom black-and-white, but I do think if you have the option to go for a long bike ride with your kids or spend the day organizing your attic, the former is the better choice. Spiritual edification is more important than cooking and cleaning, a point Jesus made to Mary and Martha in the Gospels. Comforting a teen after a rough high school dance is more important than finishing the dishes in the sink.

Of course, I understand that for some people, hitting Monday with empty hampers and clean floors feels like an accomplishment, much like ending the workday with an empty in-box feels satisfying, too. Some people even tell me that they can't relax if they know the house is a mess! The key thing with chores and weekends is not to focus so much on easily seen and measured goals, such as scratching everything off that grocery list, that you divert energy from your highest-value projects: nurturing your relationships, nurturing your career, nurturing yourself.

One way to do this? Designate a small chore time. Perhaps it's Saturday evening while you're waiting for a babysitter, or Friday evening right after dinner and before watching a movie. Regardless of when you choose, if you find yourself looking at a dirty floor at some other time, you can tell yourself that there's a time for cleaning floors—and now is not that time. Creating a small window also makes you more motivated to get the chores done quickly, so you can go on to the fun things.

Rethink Children's Activities

Another common weekend woe is the alleged tyranny of children's calendars. Parents complain that they'd like to use their weekends well, but the entire time is consumed by children's sports.

Often this isn't true from a numbers perspective. A weekend where one child has a four-hour baseball game and another has a four-hour swim meet sounds packed, though eight hours of sports is less than 25 percent of the time you're awake (thirty-six hours) during a sixty-hour weekend. I think what makes these events loom large is that practices and games are scheduled at certain times and involve commitments to other people. It's the same phenomenon that makes any random conference call seem larger and more important than spending an hour thinking about a business idea, even though the latter is objectively a bigger priority in your life. In workshops, I tell grown-ups to schedule in hours for top work priorities like strategic thinking or creative work, so these priorities seem like commitments alongside those conference calls we all spend too much time on. It's a good idea for leisure, too. Write alongside that four-hour baseball game on the calendar: "I will do a six-mile run along the river at 8:00 a.m." That reminds you that there are other parts to the weekend than children's sports and—as a bonus—when things are written down and scheduled, they are more likely to happen.

You can also make the most of children's activities. Make games into family outings. Pack a picnic lunch and get to know the other families so you can socialize with them. That's one reason I never mind going to birthday parties for the under-eight set. Viewed in the right light, they're a chance to nurture relationships while someone else is entertaining your kids. You can trade off with other parents to carpool for practice, use practices to score one-on-one time with your other children if you have a brood, or even just sit in your car and read or think. While her daughter is playing tennis, "I'll read through the whole Sunday *Times*," says Kirsten Bischoff, co-founder of the online scheduling service HATCHEDit.com. "I would otherwise feel like I was wasting huge amounts of time as a chauffeur. I'm still using my brain on weekends."

While stories of overscheduled children make headlines, research into children's use of time finds this is a smaller cultural phenomenon than people make it out to be. The average child spends far more time in front of screens of various sorts than she does doing sports, hobbies, religious activities, or homework. Only a small percentage of children are enrolled in multiple activities at any given time, and regardless, if your weekends feel overscheduled, this is a problem you can address. Pare down to the activities they and you enjoy most. When it comes to making the most of leisure time, depth and focus tend to bring more happiness than a scattershot approach where you never get a chance to go all in toward mastery.

Keep a (Tech) Sabbath

As for the encroachments work makes on weekends, I keep coming back to the concept of a Sabbath—a holy day for rest. In the well-known biblical narrative, God spent six days creating the earth, and then on the seventh he rested. He commanded the Israelites under Moses to "remember the Sabbath and keep it holy." Big chunks of the books of the law spell out what one can and cannot do on the Sabbath, and it's something Orthodox Jews are often defined by in popular culture: a prohibition against working and, for many, driving, using electricity, and so forth, from sundown Friday until sundown Saturday.

Christians have often viewed the Jewish Sabbath rules as legalistic. In Mark 2:27, after the Pharisees have complained about Jesus's disciples picking grain on the holy day, Jesus explains to them that "the Sabbath was made for man, and not man for the Sabbath."

But our distaste for the legalism may stem partly from how comfortable we are. Many of the prohibited tasks, like driving and shopping, aren't that unpleasant. Contrast this to the worldview described in Exodus 23:12, where the rule is "on the seventh day do not work, so that your ox and your donkey may rest and the slave born in your household, and the alien as well, may be refreshed." Picture the brutally hard life of a slave—and then ponder the social importance of powerful people believing that God would sit in judgment on them for making their human chattels work without a break.

It's a mind-set that perhaps some people in demanding jobs now would appreciate, because you don't have to be religious to see the benefit in not doing your normal work for at least one day a week. Perhaps the Sabbath is made for man—and man turns out to need a time for renewal. As author Joshua Foer told Gretchen Rubin on her *Happiness Project* blog about one of his major happiness secrets, "I keep the Jewish Sabbath, which is not something I did when I was eighteen. For twenty-five hours each week, everything gets turned off. No e-mail. No phone. I don't make anything. I don't destroy anything. No matter how much stress I have in my life, it all evaporates on Friday night."

Rinna Sak lives in Toronto and is a partner in a major accounting firm. She's an Orthodox Jew and observes the Sabbath. "It's very common in my field, during the busy season, for people to work seven days a week," she says. This will go on for two to three months. When she was "fresh out of university it was tough to go to senior managers and say, 'I can't work on Saturdays.' That was a tough thing to do." But here's the thing— like the wandering Israelites who didn't starve despite manna not falling from heaven on the seventh day, "I didn't get any less done. If anything, I got more done than my peers." She was always rated at the top of her class. She made partner working substantially fewer hours than others. She credits this reduced workweek with her success. "I knew that at four thirty on Friday I was leaving. I wasn't just futzing around. There were always time wasters, but I just knew that I had to get something done, so I was lightning focused. Other people just can't maintain that. You can't maintain that seven days a week, twelve hours a day." That's why, when she moved up the ranks, "I made it a rule on my jobs. Everybody got one day off on the weekend." Because of this, "my teams have always operated at a pretty optimal level. They have time to decompress."

A stretch of time apart from the computer, phone, and work stresses creates space for other things in life. Sak's Sabbaths more closely resemble the cross-training we talked about earlier than complete rest. There are Shabbat services and then get-togethers for meals with friends. Parents never get a real break from parenting and Sak has three little ones, which means that, for a day of rest, "it's really not restful." But the good thing about a Sabbath is that the kids can't spend the time Mom has off from work locked in their rooms playing video games. With a twenty-four-hour break from technology, they have to spend the time together. "It forces you to have a different kind of relationship with your spouse, your friends, your children," she says. Left to her own devices she might work around the clock, but while she answers the question "Does God really care if I use my BlackBerry?" with "Probably not," the reality is that it "forces an environment on that day for me." And that break makes a big career and a big family possible.

Even if you don't have religious prohibitions against working, you might try carving out periods of time on the weekend when you don't check your devices. Plenty of successful people do wind up working on weekends, but I was struck, in interviews, by how people tried to keep it under control. Harsh Patel, who did a two-year Teach for America stint at PFC Omar E. Torres charter school in Chicago, told me, "Coming back from work on Friday, I didn't want to do anything, so I didn't. But I found myself wasting Saturday mornings sleeping in too long, so I started getting up earlier and finishing my work—which allowed me to do whatever I wanted worry-free Saturday night and Sunday." That kept him "sane enough to teach for two years."

Bill McGowan, the television correspondent, says, "I try not to be checking e-mail every ninety minutes on the weekends." Instead, like Patel, he gets up on Saturday mornings to take care of some things. He makes himself and his wife coffee and then "I have just this really lovely, enjoyable spot on this porch we have. I take my coffee and my laptop, and—this is like seven thirty, eight in the morning—just dive in, and try to get my in-box down." Because the time isn't as fragmented, "I think a little more creatively in terms of new business to go after." This ninety-minute bout of work is made better by the delightful scenery: "I lift my eyes from the screen to see a woodpecker." There's a nice breeze and "I try to make it a very relaxing, peaceful, tranquil setting." He knows that if he takes care of lingering work in a short burst, "it eliminates the nagging and gnawing that stays somewhere in the back of your mind the whole weekend." (Incidentally, he throws many of the e-mails he writes into the draft folder to avoid people e-mailing him back later in the day and then expecting a re-sponse. "I don't want to reinforce that I'm doing a seven-day week," he says. The e-mails will go out early Monday morning.)

Just as with chores, compressing professional work into a small time frame on weekends lets you relax the rest of the time, knowing that there is a time for work, and now is not that time. The rest of the time can be Sabbath mode. Without the distractions of the Internet, you may find ideas rushing at you. I find that I get an amazing volume of ideas in church. I don't go there to brainstorm, but we get very few chances in our distracted world to just sit and be still. The one major challenge to unplugging? In the smartphone age, our cell phones come with an in-box attached. You may have your phone with you so your teen can call you to pick her up at her friend's house, but once you've got the phone you can see if you have new messages in your in-box. It's tempting to do a quick check—which breaks the spell. One quick way around this? Hide the in-box icon if you find that the spirit is willing but the flesh is weak.

HOW TO WIN
THE WEEK AHEAD

In the section on planning weekends, we talked about how important it was to schedule something fun or meaningful for Sunday night. This stretches out the weekend and focuses the mind on the pleasure you're about to experience, rather than whatever stresses are waiting for you Monday morning.

But after you have friends over for an early dinner, volunteer with Jacob Lee at the motel in Orange County, or have a massage like the Barefoot Contessa, you still have one more thing to do to secure your weekend's awesome status: carve out at least a few minutes to plan the week ahead. Schedule not just what you *have* to do, but what you *want* to do.

In *The 7 Habits of Highly Effective People*, the late Stephen Covey called this "putting first things first." He suggests an exercise that involves thinking of the roles that matter to you. I'm a writer, a wife, a mother, a runner, a friend, and a volunteer as the president of the board of directors of the Young New Yorkers' Chorus. If your list of roles starts getting unwieldy, you could compress them into the major categories: career, relationships, and self (which includes exercise, hobbies, and anything that moves your soul). Then think of your top two or three priorities in each area that you'd like to accomplish over the next 168 hours. Block these priorities into your calendar first. Once you do this, you'll likely notice something. First, blocking six to nine priorities into a 168-hour week still leaves a lot of blank space. But second, if you accomplished all those things, you would have an absolutely amazing week. Frank Baxter, former CEO of the investment bank Jefferies and former ambassador to Uruguay, does Covey's "first things first" exercise most weeks and describes it as "invaluable." On Sundays, he sits down and looks at the calendar in order to "prioritize the coming period and to leave room to be flexible to negotiate the unexpected."

Dominique Schurman, the CEO of Papyrus, likewise designates Sunday afternoons as "my planning time, to regroup and get myself organized for the upcoming week." Once the week starts, "things just start coming at me," so she needs to keep her top priorities in mind and map out her battle plan of when those things will get accomplished. "Otherwise, the time just gets eaten up by other people's requirements encroaching on my time."

What should your priorities be? Anything you like, of course, but I find it helps to have weekly goals that make progress toward annual goals—those things you'd mention in an end-of-year performance review or in that wretched genre of literature known as the family holiday letter. Try writing both of these in January for the coming December. What would you like to say you've done by the end of the year in the major categories of life? What would you like to accomplish for your career, in your relationships, and for yourself? Then break down these goals into smaller steps, and try to incorporate at least one of these steps into your weekly plan.

The reason to do this on Sunday is that if you wake up on Monday morning without a plan, you can easily lose the day as you figure it out. You burn up willpower deciding, rather than diving in before your focus is lost. I find that making a priority list for the coming week helps me end the weekend and start the new week with a sense of purpose. I'm not just flailing, or if I am, the flailing at least has some forward motion.

ALL THERE IS

In the busyness of daily life, it can seem like there will always be another weekend, but, like all things, time is finite. If you live to be eighty, you'll have a grand total of 4,160 weekends in your biography. There are probably at least that many things you'd like to do or experience during your life. Some must wait for vacations, but it's hard to cram all your desires and achievements into two or three weeks per year. While we often crash into weekends feeling overwhelmed, the impulse to do nothing leads, as one reader told me, to feeling like we're missing out on our own lives.

I was thinking of this upon seeing a round of story ideas recently on "simplifying Christmas." In the narrative these experts and companies were invoking, we're so overworked and put-upon that we should just trim the holidays to the necessities. Relax. Slow down. You don't have to bake, or throw parties, or curl the ribbon on the pile of presents stacking up under what is hopefully a minimalist tree.

Reading these ideas, I could see the wisdom in some tempering. Certainly, there's no point in filling the holidays with things that don't bring you joy and expensive stuff that no one wants.

But if you've got young kids, it doesn't take long to realize that there won't be many Christmas seasons when the little ones will race downstairs in the morning to see what Santa brought. They won't always be eager to bake with you, spilling flour on the counter in their excitement. Eventually they won't care if you don't put up a giant tree or go caroling or make hot chocolate. They'll allow you to beg off making a snowman because you're tired. But there are only a few winters—and only a few days each winter when it's snowy and you all are home together—that your children will ask to make snowmen with you. Someday, perhaps, you will be staring at the snow from the too-simple room of a hospital or nursing home, dreaming of the days when making snowmen with your children was an option. This realization leads to a different question than that suggested by all these tips on simplifying the holidays. Namely, what are you saving your energy for? This is all there is. Anything could happen and you are not guaranteed another snowman. So make a fuss. Make a show. Spend your energy now.

It's the same with weekends, which are miniature versions of the holidays we struggle to optimize. It is always easier to do "nothing" (meaningless somethings) and do only the things we have to do. Cast loose from the schedule of work and school, we list around. We don't think about what we'd like to do with our time, and so we live a constrained version of life.

But we can choose differently. I am writing this right after Labor Day weekend on a drizzly, dreary Tuesday as my backyard is a mash of overgrown green. The leaves, though, are already turning mottled yellow at the edges. September brings a melancholy sense of time passing, as my oldest child is off to kindergarten, the three-year-old starts preschool, and even the baby turns daily into a little girl who laughs and stumbles toward her first steps. In the photos from last Labor Day she was simply a very round belly. Now we've gotten to know the sweet, toddling child once contained in that roundness.

I hadn't been planning anything special for Labor Day weekend, but it seemed a shame not to wring every last drop from summer. And so my family wound up taking a road trip to the coast and the mountains—through Ocean City, Maryland, with its Ferris wheels and margaritas, and on through the Manassas battlefields in Virginia, and ultimately out to Shenandoah National Park. As we wound our way down Skyline Drive, we paused to hike any trail under two miles that the kids could handle. They relished scrambling over the rocks on one summit, looking out at the green fields, the hay bales, and shapes of other mountains bearing shadows of the clouds.

Traveling with little ones is always challenging. There are highs and lows—always in the same day, often in the same hour. In the rearview mirror, though, the experiencing self who spent forty minutes trying to get the baby to lie down in her portable crib is replaced by the remembering self. The remembering self has turned what could be fallow, forgettable days into memories sown in the brain. These memories are there to nourish that brain through its weekday labors. They are there to fortify the soul in years to come when the busyness of now is replaced by a quieter life—as quiet as an off-season amusement park when the kiddie rides have been packed up after Labor Day empties the shore.

What the most successful people know about weekends is

that life cannot happen only in the future. It cannot wait for some day when we are less tired or less busy. If you work long hours, then weekends are key to feeling like you have a life that is broader than your professional identity—even if, and probably because, you take that identity very seriously. The marathoner knows that rest days and cross-training days spur physical breakthroughs. Likewise, the mind needs to lay different pathways, needs to stretch itself to coax a nervous child to blow bubbles in the swimming pool so it can more cleverly negotiate a business deal. As you summon the willpower to pedal up that last hill, you develop the discipline to calmly lead a classroom or comfort a patient in the last minutes of a long shift. By treating the weekend part of one's 168 hours as different and precious, you can recharge the batteries and hit Monday ready to go.

WHAT THE MOST SUCCESSFUL PEOPLE

DO AT WORK

THE SECRET OF ASTONISHING PRODUCTIVITY

Deep in the countryside of Bordeaux, France, anyone out wandering one early-January night in 2013 might have caught a curious sight: a black-haired woman in a lit studio window scratching out ink drawings of the Alaskan tundra.

Outside the otherwise dark house the scene was tranquil. Inside, it was considerably noisier. Artist LeUyen Pham paints and draws best with the TV or radio on—"something to occupy the right hemisphere of my brain," she explains. "If I'm thinking too much, my paintings look horrible. They look overthought." During the afternoon, her media diet consists of *Seinfeld* or *Mad Men* reruns. At night, it's often NPR, piped in through the magic of technology to her temporary home in rural France, where she moved with her husband and five- and two-year-old sons in the summer of 2012. This particular night, she had two iPads fired up simultaneously: one was for playing a movie, and one was for "looking up things I might need at the last second—how a fabric might look, what a moose hide might look like."

Such authenticity was necessary for Pham's portraits of a fictional girl named Bo who grew up in a 1920s mining village on the Yukon River, a place depicted in hundreds of old photographs crammed into Pham's studio since she took on the project of illustrating a children's chapter book by Kirkpatrick Hill called *Bo at Ballard Creek*. The book was due out in June 2013, and so she was racing toward a deadline. "On a non-deadline day, between nine and eleven in the morning is when I flow best, when I'm most invested in my work," she says. On deadline days, though, "my best time is around eleven at night. There is absolutely no distraction to be had. You're pretty much shackled to your desk." She pauses. "There's something really nice about that."

Indeed, Pham was so captivated by this *Little House on the Prairie*–type tale, set in the far north, that although she'd originally been contracted for one illustration per chapter, she proposed dozens more ("it's a great, great story," she says). The publisher loved them all. And so night after night in January, she took to her desk for another shift, drawing energy from her drawings. At times like those, "I'm actually in heaven," she says. "I don't realize what time it is. I don't think I'm tired" until a wee-hours yawn proves otherwise.

Whether she's tired or not, Pham's schedule sounds wearying. Since starting her career at DreamWorks, and then going out on her own a decade ago, she has become one of the most prolific children's book illustrators working in the field. These days she's conjuring up eight or nine titles a year, including board books (like *Whose Toes Are Those?* written by Jabari Asim), picture books (like the *Freckleface Strawberry* books, written by actress Julianne Moore), and chapter books like *Bo at Ballard Creek*. "I know it's an insane amount. I don't know a whole lot of illustrators who do that many," she says, given that a thirty-two-page children's book can consist of, in essence, thirty-two fully executed, gallery-quality paintings. Four or five titles a year would be a full schedule for most people, and so "I'm working on multiple projects at the same time," she says. "Always."

Yet she manages to maintain high standards. Her secret? For one, she is careful with her time. "I absolutely quantify my hours," she says. She'll monitor her work to see "what have I produced in half an hour, in an hour—it's half hours to hours to days to weeks." She'll set goals for all those time periods, like giving herself one episode of *Seinfeld* (twenty-two minutes plus commercials) to finish a drawing.

That intimate knowledge of her hours means she can quickly describe what a usual workday looks like for her. She's up around 6:00 a.m., working on "thumbnail" sketches that help her plan what she'll paint or ink later. She also tackles any administrative work—e-mails with editors and the like. Her boys rise at around 7:30, so she plays with them and helps her husband get them out the door to school. Then at 8:30, it's back to work for more thinking and planning while she's still fresh. At around 10:00, she'll switch over to executing on her thumbnail sketches. That's when she puts *Seinfeld* and similar shows on, until 4:00 or 5:00 p.m., when she might try to reach people on the East Coast. After that, she turns her attention to the children again, playing with them and eating dinner. Before their bedtime, she reads them a story—sometimes one she's written, but she also uses this as a chance to check out the competition—and then it's back to work for a third shift. With the pastoral view of the Bordeaux landscape reduced to blackness outside, she starts making art almost by instinct. "It's like driving a car to a place you know so well you almost don't look where you're driving," she says.

Of course, her ability to summon that instinct is due to her other secrets of astonishing productivity. She makes time to keep improving at her craft, something she says she ponders "with every single project I get. I have so many different styles, and I try to cultivate that. When I was first in the business, people told me you've got to have a single style for which you become known. That gets you more work. But I could never get excited about that. It's so boring to paint in one particular way. Yes, you get better at one style, but you get out of your mind sick of it." In fact, "other artists cautioned me against doing that." Any one style of painting can go out of fashion, but keeping yourself a nimble student of the discipline makes learning new styles possible. "It's a lot of extra work, but it's like reinventing yourself for each book," she says.

She has learned to be creative basically on demand—even if she's tired, even if she's interrupted by family matters—by honing tactics that prime her brain. She keeps abreast of what other artists are doing; she researches things like moose hides and Alaskan fabric every time she starts a project so that the aesthetics of the world she'll depict permeate her consciousness. And when that fails, she's got other tricks in her paint pots. In December 2012, while updating a book called *There's No Such Thing As Little*, she faced such a block that she could only tiptoe through it by making Christmas ornaments. "We forgot to bring Christmas ornaments when we moved to France," she explains, so she coaxed out her creative impulses by making holiday decorations: forty carefully crafted sculptures consisting of pinecone elves, cork Santa Clauses, and cork angels. She painted a face on a hazelnut, glued black felt on it, and made a vampire. "I was really surprised at how well the tree came out," Pham says. The book got made, too, and, since she was recently offered a job illustrating a book on the twelve days of Christmas, her hours did double duty as she pondered Christmas visuals.

Indeed, all of Pham's hours seem to count multiple times. She is constantly learning new ways to illustrate as she absorbs what is around her. Even a trip to a town café can turn into art, as it did with another book coming out in the summer of 2013 called *The Boy Who Loved Math*. It's a children's book about legendarily prolific mathematician Paul Erdős. When she first got the manuscript Pham said, "You've got the wrong person." But—perhaps intrigued by Erdős's sheer quantity of output— she threw herself into learning about the man and his mathematics. She found that she loved the idea of using his beautiful proofs in the compositions themselves. One of his conjectures had to do with how many squares of different sizes could fit in a larger square; on one page, the text conveys that Paul couldn't find a way to fit into the world, that he was different from everyone else. Pham painted people sitting in a café, and each of them occupied a differently sized square. Erdős got a pentagon. The squares and shapes were all his idea, but the café was Pham's invention from wandering around France. "Everything, whatever's around me at the moment, finds its way into my work," she says.

What makes Pham's schedule possible is that she only takes on work like *Bo at Ballard Creek* or *The Boy Who Loved*

Math—work that challenges her and allows her to find joy in steady progress toward a goal she thinks matters. I ask her if she chooses stories that she can picture delighting children, and she laughs. "I would love to say that was it, but my initial attraction is that it's a project that I, myself, would love to do," she says. "I would assume in consequence that kids like it, because I have a very childlike mentality, and my kids seem to like the same stories and same ideas," but ultimately, she chooses work that she loves for its own sake. That makes near miracles possible. Her output increases as the years go on. After her friends started having kids, Pham says, many had identity crises of sorts, pondering whether their work was worth the time they put into it. But rather than scaling back, she scaled up, even as she spends many hours with her little ones, too. "I don't really care the extent of the work," she says, "if I'm sure at the end it's going to look good."

• • •

I've interviewed many people about their jobs and daily schedules over the years, but I've come back to Pham several times. I always enjoy talking to her, partly because her work is so fascinating to a book lover like myself, but also because I think she sees, clearly, both the effort success requires and how joyous work can be. The combination of the two is rare. My head spins every time I get off the phone with Pham.

Of course, few people make their living drawing mathematicians or girls who lived during the Alaskan Gold Rush, so I'm guessing your workdays look a little different from Pham's. Children's book illustrators will naturally work differently than nurses, farmers, teachers, postal clerks, corporate vice presidents, or any of the other vocations represented among the world's 7 billion souls—a fact many productivity tomes obsessed with a corporate environment miss. Nonetheless, we all face the truth that our lives are built in hours. What you will accomplish will be a function of how you spend those hours. And so the mind-set Pham has toward her hours, and, by extension, her life's work, can be transferred from the canvas of her life to anyone else's.

Many of us could use the help. As with money, we have a tendency to fritter away the time in front of us as if it were infinite. For some of us, that's because our hours are sucked into the Reply All maw of an in-box. Others, perhaps, can see that the customer who wandered into their store left with her real need unaddressed and won't be coming back. A dentist sees that a patient didn't absorb her halfhearted pep talk on flossing and knows that the patient will be back soon for more fillings and another tepid pep talk. We find ourselves counting minutes and wishing ourselves elsewhere. These hours pass, inexorably, with little promise of leading to much that matters. They are spent and the transaction is done, like paying a late fee on a cell phone bill or buying a sweater that you never wind up wearing.

But as with money, people who build wealth take some chunk of what is coming in and invest it in ways that generate returns. Successful people know that hours, like capital, can be consciously allocated with the goal of creating riches—in the form of a changed world, a life's work—over time. Indeed, successful people understand that work hours must be more carefully stewarded than capital because time is absolutely limited. You can earn more money, but the mightiest among us is granted no more than 168 hours per week, and it is physically impossible to work for all of them.

If you make certain choices in your work, though, if you develop certain disciplines and invest your time instead of squandering it, you can do more with the time you have. Pham describes it as a sort of magical thinking. "I cannot understand how I produce the amount of work I do in the time I have. My husband says, 'You have a carefully constructed sense of self-delusion,' which is totally true." But no matter how deluded the deadlines are—she jokes that she'd be tempted to take a project requiring one hundred paintings in three and a half days—"between eleven and two, when I'm on a roll and inspired and it's just coming out, I don't even know how to quantify time anymore. I'm whipping through it and it feels really, really lovely."

How do you build your career so that hard work feels lovely? How can you spend your hours to make a prodigious amount of your best work possible? How can you invest your time so that your work then speaks for you, multiplying what you can do on your own? How can you experience the joy of doing what you feel matters?

These are difficult questions. They may also be depressing questions if you frequently find yourself stuck in meetings that run long past the point of diminishing returns. The good news is there are lots of ways to start tending your time more carefully. Even if you think you lack complete control of your time, and even if you feel battered by the gales of creative destruction swirling through the economy, you can look at your calendar and see the possibilities inherent in minutes rather than seeing them as sands sifting through an hourglass. The secret to astonishing productivity lies in a handful of daily disciplines that, as Pham and other successful people have discovered, have the power to make work hours count more. "I will never get over the fact that I'm super lucky to be in this position," she says. "My kids can see that I love what I do."

MIND YOUR HOURS

I first came to the topic of time not because I was interested in time management but because I was fascinated by the academic study of time use. Hunting through data from the American Time Use Survey, conducted annually by the Bureau of Labor Statistics, and other time diary projects, I came to the inescapable conclusion that how we think we spend our time has little to do with reality. We wildly overestimate time devoted to housework. We underestimate time devoted to sleep. We write whole treatises glorifying a golden age that never was; American women, for instance, spend more time with their children now than their grandmothers did in the 1950s and '60s.

These curious blind spots continue into the realm of work. People who get paid by the hour know how many hours they work. People who inhabit the world of exempt jobs have a much more tenuous grasp on this concept but, as a general rule, the higher the number of work hours reported, the more likely the person is to be overestimating. A study published in the June 2011 *Monthly Labor Review* that compared estimated workweeks with time diaries reported that people who claimed their "usual" workweeks were longer than 75 hours were off, on average, by about twenty-five hours. You can guess in which direction. Those who claimed that a "usual" work-week was 65–74 hours were off by close to twenty hours. Those claiming a 55–64 hour workweek were still about ten hours north of the truth. Subtracting these errors, you can see that most people top out at fewer than sixty work hours per week. Many professionals in so-called extreme jobs work about 45–55 hours per week. Those are numbers I can attest to from time logs I've seen over the years. I've given speeches at com-panies known for their sweatshop hours and had up-and-comers keep time logs for me. Their recorded weeks tend to hover around sixty hours—and that's for focused, busy weeks with no half days, vacation days, or dentist appointments, and, most important, for weeks that people are willing to share with colleagues. We live in a competitive world, and boasting about the number of hours we work has become a way to demonstrate how devoted we are to our jobs.

That would be funny, except that numbers have conse-quences. If you think you're working eighty hours per week, you'll make different choices in your attempts to optimize them than if you know you usually work fifty-five. That's why Pham is careful to quantify her hours, and it's why people who want to use their hours better figure out how they're spending their hours now. If you've ever tried to lose weight, you know that nutritionists will tell you to keep a food journal, because evidence shows it works. One study of a year-long weight-loss program, published in the *Journal of the Academy of Nutrition and Dietetics* in 2012, found that women who kept a food jour-nal lost about six pounds more than those who did not. Writ-ing down what you eat keeps you accountable for what you put in your mouth. Likewise, writing down how you spend your time keeps you accountable for the hours that pass, whether or not you're conscious of them.

There are lots of apps that can help you keep a time log, or you can download a decidedly low-tech spreadsheet from my website.* I use the even-lower-tech solution of writing down my hours in a spiral notebook. If you've never kept track of your time before, I encourage you to try logging a whole week and think of yourself as a lawyer billing time to different projects. How much time do you spend checking e-mail? Thinking? Planning? Traveling? In meetings? Doing the substance of whatever work you were hired to do?

Tally up the totals and study them. Do those totals seem reasonable? What do you over- or underinvest in? Perhaps the most important insight to come out of this experiment is an understanding of exactly how long activities take. If I've got a blog post written, it takes me a half hour to format it with links and photos—a good thing to know before attempting to post between the 11:45 a.m. end of a phone call and lunch with my kids at noon. People who do a lot of something often develop a good sense for this, and consequently have a more accurate understanding of how much they can produce in the 2,000–3,000 annual work hours that a 40–60-hour workweek entails. For Pham, a painting takes a certain number of *Seinfeld* episodes. An October 2012 *Wall Street Journal* profile of Connie Brown, an artist who specializes in personalized maps, reported that a map took her more than two hundred hours to complete, and so she did about twelve a year. Even

---

* http://lauravanderkam.com/books/168-hours/manage-your-time/

adding administrative time, that puts her in the 2,000–3,000-hour bucket. A less experienced artist might attempt to tackle fifty such projects per year, but since that's 10,000 hours, and a year has just 8,760 hours (8,784 during leap years), that clearly wouldn't work.

You don't have to log your minutes forever, but even doing it for a few days gives you a mindfulness about time—a mindfulness I imagine monastic sorts were pursuing as they meditated through their books of hours. That mindfulness can lead to more productive choices by itself. One busy doctor who kept a time log for me subsequently took her log to her clinic director to make the case for more administrative support so she could see more patients. Having logged many weeks over the years, I no longer propose phone calls before 11:00 a.m. if I get a say in the matter. That's because I know that morning hours are when I am best able to turn an idea into words.

You may be frustrated to discover that how you're spending your time isn't how you wish to be spending your time, but the stark truth is that time is a nonrenewable resource—when it's gone, it's gone. There is no point lamenting how many of your hours have been lost in the past. There is much to be gained, though, by committing to doing things differently in the 2,000–3,000 work hours you are granted as a blank slate each year.

PLAN

Once you know how many work hours you have available to you, the next step for transforming your career is figuring out what you'd like to do with them. Teachers' contracts often allow for a planning period so they can set objectives and create lessons in a time separate from their "on" hours in front of children. It doesn't always work, but having that designated time creates a culture where thinking through what you intend to do before you do it is possible. Erica Woolway, the chief academic officer of Uncommon Schools and coauthor with Doug Lemov and Katie Yezzi of *Practice Perfect: 42 Rules for Getting Better at Getting Better*, studied effective teachers and found that they were "really, in a detailed way, scripting out lesson plans, scripting out questions you will ask students. That type of planning is a big distinguishing factor between the good teachers and the not-so-great."

But when's the last time you gave yourself a planning period? When I poll audiences about what they'd like to spend more time on, planning and thinking land near the top of the list. People lament that they'd love to have strategic-thinking time, but they're just too busy! This always strikes me as a bit backward. You hope whoever is building your house isn't so busy hammering and sawing that he can't look at the blue-print. Likewise, successful people—who have the same 168 hours per week as the rest of us—simply build planning into their lives. Pham's thumbnail sketches help her and her publishers decide the order of panels and what each one will contain. It would not make sense to attempt thirty-two sequentially related paintings without thinking through what will be in them. It would be a colossal waste of time to start a painting only to realize halfway through that the cloud would look much better on the left side of the moon.

Design is half the battle, and this is true in business contexts, too. The Executive Time Use Project, run out of the London School of Economics and Political Science, has had executive assistants keep track of CEO time use at publicly listed companies in multiple countries. Preliminary analysis from CEOs in India found that a firm's sales increased as the CEO worked more hours. But more intriguingly, the correlation between CEO time use and output was driven entirely by hours spent in planned activities. Planning doesn't have to mean that the hours are spent in meetings, though meetings with employees were correlated with higher sales; it's just that CEO time is a limited and valuable resource, and planning how it should be allocated increases the chances that it's spent in productive ways.

This is the thinking behind Michael Soenen's work ritual of a weekend planning period. Soenen was the CEO of FTD (the florist network) for years and now runs EmergencyLink, a company that stores emergency information in a way that's accessible to family and first responders. He says that his most important personal habit is to carve out the back half of

Sunday for strategic thinking. He spends a few hours considering "what are our priorities, and I make sure those priorities are distributed to the team. I think through any questions I have, what are the important projects. If those are made clear Sunday night, coming into Monday morning, everyone really knows what to do." The team can have a quick call Monday morning and go. Such planning makes the whole week more productive, says Soenen, because his role, as a leader, is "to help my people be as efficient as possible with their time. It's hard for them to be efficient if you don't think, institutionally, what are the best ideas." If he waits until Monday morning to plan, then it's not until Monday afternoon that people figure out what they need to do, and he risks his people running hard in the wrong direction. If you've got ten people working for you, four haphazard hours on Monday morning means forty misdirected hours. That's like losing a full-time equivalent from your staff. But if Soenen has a great Sunday afternoon, then everyone else has a great week. "For me, I've noticed when I spend that time it makes a big difference," he says.

Devotees of David Allen's GTD system—which stands for "Getting Things Done"—carve out time for a weekly review. During this time, they look at loose ends, put things on the "someday/maybe" list, and define the next actions required on big projects. Allen himself finds that "the end of the week is a nice time to do it," or on Sundays or on long plane trips. "That's a good time to sit down and do that kind of back-off thinking." The key is finding a time and place where "the world kind of slows down, the phones aren't ringing, people aren't pinging me instantly while I'm at my desk." Since some of his clients almost never experience a slowdown like that, he reports that some of them don't schedule anything before 9:00 a.m. so they can start at 7:00 a.m. and "get zeroed out before the madness." Some of them decide to work at home on Fridays and use the first half of the day for reflection time so they can review their weeks without the world clawing at them at the office. Whatever you choose, get everything out of your brain and figure out unfinished business. "I don't want to add any new creative stuff on top of stuff that's stale," says Allen, but with work defined, he can then welcome new ideas and ponder what's next.

I tend to do my own planning on three levels. Each December, I think of questions I'd ask in the "performance review" I hope to give myself at the end of the next calendar year. What would I like to accomplish in my next two thousand working hours? To be sure, the future is unknowable, and goals can be changed. Nonetheless, setting annual goals—such as "double my blog traffic" or "write a draft of a novel"—focuses my brain on actions that would help achieve those goals. With my annual goals in mind, I then make a priority list every Sunday night of what I plan to accomplish in the next week. That priority list will include both immediate assignments and steps toward my annual goals (like "study Google Analytics for 30 minutes to see what drives traffic" and "write 2,000 words of fiction"). I tightly schedule Monday and loosely schedule the rest of the week. Then on Monday night I schedule Tuesday more tightly, based on what's left on the priority list and what's come up on Monday. Tuesday night I schedule Wednesday, and so forth. I've usually gotten most things done by Friday, which can be a mop-up day or a time for more planning.

People work in different ways, so there is no one version of planning that will work for everyone. If you work very closely with another person—an assistant, for instance, or the librettist who writes the words for all your operas—that person will need to participate in some of your planning. If you have many requests for specific chunks of your time, your planning might require more careful scripting than if your work culture permits wandering into a colleague's office and spending four hours debating a mathematical proof. The important thing is not so much the format. It's getting in the habit of scheduling a planning period. Once you get in the rhythm of planning, though, of thinking through things before you do them, you'll find it's quite addictive. You might start working at strange times just to be sure you get your planning fix. Durval Tavares, CEO of Aquabotix, a company that makes underwater robots, confesses that he's sometimes up at 4:00 a.m. "not because of the alarm," but because he has lots of things on his mind. "You want clarity," he says. "It's hard once you get into your office to have a moment to just think and strategize and figure out things." So he plans before breakfast and comes to work ready to face the day.

You might also start planning your personal life. Mike Williams, a former executive at GE who is now the CEO of the David Allen Company, reports that he spends a few minutes at the end of the workday reviewing what he'd like to focus on in the evenings. For instance, he'll mark on his calendar that his daughter had a presentation that day: "Ask her how it went." That way, when he walks in the door, he's truly present for his family. As he notes, he has just four more years before his teenager leaves home, and he sees the chance for communication and to do special activities together as "gems I don't want to lose. In the past, if I didn't write those down, I'd miss those opportunities." As with work hours, leisure and family hours pass whether or not you think through how you intend to spend them. Knowing where you're going vastly increases the chances that you'll get there.

MAKE SUCCESS POSSIBLE

Once you start scheduling regular planning sessions, you'll gather all sorts of kindling for lighting a fire under your career. You'll think of a hundred new people you want to meet. You'll think of a hundred new ideas for growing your business. But, as counterintuitive as it sounds, resist the temptation to put all these wonderful ideas on the to-do list for Monday. Pace yourself. Successful people tend to view their primary to-do lists a bit differently than others do. They aren't just lists. They're more like contracts. Whatever is on the list will get done, often as a matter of personal pride. This is true even if your deadlines turn out to be squishy. Pham, for instance, reports that "in the past year, I think my publishers thought I'd slow down with my second kid, but I keep hitting all these deadlines." Now, a few projects are in a dormant phase as she waits for other people to catch up.

Since life comes up and emergencies happen, making success possible hinges on two things: being choosy about each day's priority list and developing an accountability system that works.

Chalene Johnson, the fitness personality best known for creating the Turbo Jam exercise videos, tends to limit her daily priority list to six items: three things that must get done that day, and three small steps toward what she calls her "push" goal for the year. This is a measurable goal whose achievement would make her other big goals possible. Sometimes that means it's not her most obvious goal. For instance, in 2011, she wanted her book, *Push: 30 Days to Turbocharged Habits, a Bangin' Body, and the Life You Deserve!* to hit the bestseller list. That's a goal in its own right, but she realized that the key to making that happen was to accumulate at least 100,000 fan e-mail addresses so she could reach out and market to these people. The promotional activities necessary to create that database became her push goal. Another push goal? Roughly a year before we talked, she sold two of her companies to Beachbody, the home fitness company. She stayed on as a consultant for a year, with part of her payout hinging on Beachbody's success. So that year's push goal was helping Beachbody hit a solid level of profit. The day I interviewed Johnson, one of the three steps was to set up an appointment with a man she was working with on a project. The second was to set up a teleconference with the CEO for the next day. The third was to revise an outline for a presentation.

Getting through the list is "pretty easy when you only have six things," she says. "I breeze through them and feel very accomplished. It creates an adrenaline rush, a snowball effect for me to want to stay on a roll." Indeed, "the reasoning behind limiting, editing your list to fewer items, is you never feel defeated. You got everything done that had to get done. Most people think they have to sprint and that's why they never hit their big push goals—because they run out of steam." Doing three things per day in pursuit of a big goal may not seem like much, but doing three things every workday without fail could put you 750 steps closer to your goal in a year. If your goal for the year is to write a 75,000-word manuscript, each small step could be writing a mere 100 words—less than the length of this paragraph—and you'd easily hit that. Successful people know that small things done repeatedly have great power.

Like Johnson, David Allen limits his list. After glancing over the "hard landscape" of his day—getting familiar with appointments and the like—he says that, "given the potential discretionary time, I choose one, two, or maybe three things I'm going to focus on." He tells people to aim for the small number, and then "if you say, 'Wow, I got all that stuff done,' and you have any more time, great, go pick some more. But don't overwhelm yourself." People have a tendency to, "after coffee, totally overcommit."

Johnson increases her chances of success not only by limiting her list but by developing habits that ensure accountability. She creates certain mental triggers—for instance, if she sees the number 11 somewhere—to check her list. "My to-do list is on my phone," she says, and if an item on her to-do list is as simple as sending a text message, she can do that while she's standing in line at the grocery store. "It's a no-fail situation," she says.

Another way to build in accountability is to join an accountability group or to choose an accountability partner. Nika Stewart, who owns a New Jersey–based social media marketing business called Ghost Tweeting, is part of the 7-Figure Club, an accountability group sponsored by the Savor the Success network of women business owners. Every

Monday, each entrepreneur checks in online to set a weekly goal that will advance her toward her annual goals. Then on Friday everyone checks back in to say if she did or didn't do it. If Stewart's weekly goal, stated on Monday, was to send out ten proposals, "Thursday night, if I didn't do it, I might stay up and do it," she says.

No one wants to look like a failure in front of people whose opinions they value.

This insight led to the creation of one of my favorite business concepts, an organization called stickK.* Users set goals to stop smoking, work out regularly, lose weight, or a host of other things. To ensure accountability, a person signs a commitment contract, which states his goal, and then he can put a financial wager on achieving that goal. He also produces a list of supporters who will be kept apprised of his progress. If you, as a stickK user, slip up and grab a soda when you have vowed not to, your money might go to a designated person or even an "anti-charity," which is one whose values you don't support (think along the lines of Karl Rove's super PAC if you're a liberal Democrat). Your friends will also be informed of your failure. "Not only are you challenging yourself by saying, 'Hey, I can do this,' you're also putting your reputation at stake," says stickK's FAQs. Research from stickK's founders has found that commitment contracts along these lines more than triple a person's chances of success.

Successful people understand that willpower is great, but it is also a virtue many of us possess in limited supply. Your boss

---

* http://www.stickk.com

will keep you accountable to some goals, but if you've got broader goals, or if you don't have a boss, you'll need a secondary system. Figure out what app, website, person, financial wager, or group will make failure as uncomfortable as possible, and use that to make your goals happen.

KNOW WHAT IS WORK

From time to time I am contacted by companies that make time-tracking software, which is generally designed for employers who wish to discourage employees from goofing off. Often these pitches feature intriguing statistics such as "Businesses lose nearly $1.1 billion a week in time spent on fantasy football teams." Monitor your employees' time to see how many minutes feature screens full of ESPN instead of Outlook and—boom!—productivity will go through the roof! Right?

Well, maybe. I seldom write about such programs because, aside from the Big Brother aspect, the truth is that most professionals don't consider spending eight hours a day watching cat videos on YouTube as a good use of time. You may do a quick check of your fantasy football team's status after an intense meeting, but this wastes, maybe, a few minutes, and no one is under any delusion that this is "work." A more insidious problem—a problem that drains far more cash than the $1.1 billion allegedly lost each week to fantasy football—lies in the things that look like work, but aren't actually work. They may, theoretically, be part of your job, but they're not work if they're not advancing you or your organization toward your goals.

Take e-mail. According to a 2012 McKinsey Global Institute report on the social economy, knowledge workers spend 28 percent of their time wading through their in-boxes. According to Lookout, the mobile-security firm, 58 percent of smartphone users say they don't go an hour without checking their phones. And not just waking hours. Lookout reported that 54 percent of smartphone users check their phones while lying in bed. Almost 40 percent say they check their phones while on the toilet. Some 9 percent admit to checking their phones during religious services. Much of this constant connectivity is about checking e-mail, and e-mail certainly looks like work. But if checking e-mail ten times per hour means that writing a presentation takes two hours instead of one, it's hard to say that was a better use of time than writing for thirty minutes, checking e-mail for fifteen, writing for another thirty minutes, then watching cat videos for forty-five minutes straight. And if some of those e-mails didn't need to be read at all—think of how many threads you delete after coming back from vacation—then you would have done just as well to cruise over to your fantasy football website while you were at it.

Or consider that bane of white-collar existence, meetings, and their remote-work sibling, conference calls. I'm often astonished by the sheer volume of meetings that show up on people's time logs. Jackie Pyke, vice president for brand strategy and governance at Capital One, estimates her meeting load is 70 percent of her schedule, "And it could be 100 percent if I let it and if I did not actively manage who is making meeting requests. We're an extremely inclusive and collaborative culture, so people err on the side of including lots of people."

Collaboration is wonderful, but it has a downside because the volume of meetings soon turns into a vicious cycle. The best way to get people to pay attention to a project is to schedule a meeting—because meetings become deadlines. If you don't schedule a meeting, your project will fall behind the other six meetings people have for that day in the priority list. That's not because your project is objectively less important. It's because things that happen at a specific time and involve commitments to other people automatically seem more important than they are.

To be sure, people do need to meet, just like they need to send and read e-mail, and in many cases, meetings—at least the one-on-one sorts—are critical to good management. What successful people do is to constantly calculate the opportunity cost. Pyke says, "I challenge myself once a year or more to study how I'm spending my time and see if I can make some game-changing moves." She'll clear the calendar of meetings scheduled in perpetuity, so those meetings have to earn their way back into her life. She'll look at meetings she used to think she had to be in and ask, "How could I not be there? Maybe it's uncomfortable, but it presents an opportunity for someone else on my team to step up." Or sometimes she'll notice that someone is already stepping up—and that's a red flag that she doesn't need to be there. Her team members are smart people, and they can probably handle it. Of course, part of working with good people involves meeting with them and supporting their development. "I really try to protect an hour a week with each of my direct reports," Pyke says, but she realizes "that's not realistic for me or them. They're moving up in seniority as well. An hour a week is a lot. They're much more autonomous than when they were at the more junior level." Maybe the check-in should be an hour every other week.

Or you can block an hour but not take an hour. Colin Day, CEO of iCIMS, an HR software company, has time in his calendar to meet for an hour, weekly, with each of his five direct reports at his 250-person company, but says they "don't feel the need to hang around for an hour because it's an hour." Nothing makes him happier than to get everything clarified in five minutes, or just via instant messaging. Then he and they can go recapture that time—because successful people are always asking some version of the question "What else could I do with that hour?" A good reason to mind your hours and to know how long things take is that you can then translate any given request for your time into those terms. You know that calling six old clients—and spending twenty minutes on the phone with them apiece—is quite likely to result in at least one request for a proposal. A two-hour meeting is thus the equivalent of giving up a good lead on new work. Is it worth that? Or could the meeting take only an hour, giving you the other hour to reach out? Sometimes it helps to put this question in terms of cold, hard cash. A recurring meeting that involves ten people getting together for two hours per week costs the same as having another part-timer on staff. Are you getting as much value out of that two-hour meeting as another employee would add? Or are the first fifteen minutes critical, and the rest is just a voluntary tax on your organization's time?

This question of opportunity cost is particularly important if you're running a small business. Entrepreneurs often have a terrible time delegating the tasks they know they're good at, but the problem with having just 2,000–3,000 work hours per year is that a choice to write the first draft of that report yourself, because you have a zesty way with verbs, is a choice not to figure out which of your revenue streams is growing fastest and deserves more attention. Those who leap from microbusiness to million-dollar business tend to make this calculation. Traci Bild's Bild and Company provides consulting services for senior housing companies. The organization generates $4 million in revenue each year, yet Bild leaves work at 3:00 p.m. to tackle the after-school shift at home. Her secret? "I'm constantly trying to replace myself," she says. "In my work, my number one strategy as a leader is to replace myself. If I give my duties away, it frees me up to go to the next level. That's been my strategy for years and it's worked incredibly well."

Josh Skolnick, a twentysomething entrepreneur, started mowing lawns in high school in suburban Philadelphia. He was so entrepreneurial that by the time he graduated, he had multiple crews working for him. He decided to go into tree care and trimming after sensing it was a profitable market. A client asked him to deal with a dead tree, so Skolnick hired a contractor and, since the guy was there, started knocking on doors to see if the neighbors needed any tree services, too. He sold $20,000 worth of work in a day. Clearly, Skolnick is very good at retail selling. But as he continues to build the company that became Monster Tree Service into a national franchise, it no longer makes as much sense for him to go knocking on doors, even though he does it well. So he's trained his crew foremen to walk around properties with homeowners and point out looming limbs and potential rot. He's also trained them to say hello to neighbors who are out in their yards and make soft sales that way. "People will shock you. It's amazing what people are capable of doing," he says. "I've got guys working for me who I'd never guess would be able to sell tree work," but they've learned and mastered it and generated thousands of dollars in sales, which Skolnick makes sure to reward them for. "What I find with my business is that I gain respect from employees when I treat them as I would want to be treated," he says. "From a financial perspective, I take care of my employees and provide a bonus structure to incentivize them to accept more responsibility."

Of course, in your quest to make sure you don't mistake things that look like work for actual work, there's a corollary, which is that you shouldn't fail to see as "work" things that really are. Productivity involves working with your temporal body, as opposed to against it. All kinds of things that don't look like work, when viewed from the right angle, are in fact great uses of time.

For most of us, that means activities like taking breaks. Pham gets up and does yoga stretches every hour. I'll go for a walk or a run or out to do an errand during my low-energy time in the afternoon. I know that if I stay at my computer, I'm likely to find myself drifting over to e-mail every thirty seconds rather than cranking things out. Curiously, these breaks often enable me to process ideas that haven't quite fit together during my active work time. While writing this part of the book, I considered canceling a six-mile jog with my running partner because I was falling behind on my deadline. But I went and hashed out the outline with her as we puffed along. Perhaps it didn't look like work. But I got a lot more done than I would have sitting at my desk.

Some research finds that such breaks—and general self-care—have a fairly strong financial return. In 2006, Tony Schwartz and Catherine McCarthy studied productivity at several Wachovia bank branches in New Jersey. They put 106 employees through a four-month wellness program that involved instruction on energy management, with guidelines for eating regularly, defusing negative emotions, and getting up from their desks from time to time. Compared with a control group, the energy management group achieved a 13 percentage point greater increase in revenue from loans and a 20 percentage point greater increase in revenue from deposits on a year-over-year basis. (As Schwartz and McCarthy pointed out in their 2007 *Harvard Business Review* write-up of the study, Wachovia used those metrics to evaluate employees.) To be sure, it's hard to know exactly what motivates a person. A wellness program may simply make someone believe that her boss cares about her as a person—and that's the key motivating factor, not the program itself. That said, plenty of people who've tried scheduling regular breaks have found that the time "lost" is more than made up for with renewed focus.

Matt Hall builds such breaks into the culture of Hill Investment Group, a wealth management firm in Saint Louis. Hall cofounded Hill Investment Group in 2005 with the goal of helping clients to "take the long view." Good investing is about achieving maximum sustainable returns—with the emphasis on sustainable—and likewise, Hall tries to manage his hours like he manages his clients' money: carefully.

The week as a whole, and the hours within it, are well choreographed. On Monday and Friday he does the work of scheduling and prepping so that he can focus on clients on

Tuesday, Wednesday, and Thursday. Hall knows that 10:00 a.m. to noon are his peak-focus hours, so, he says, "I treat it like real estate. What's the most valuable real estate you have? You wouldn't just give it away." The week is scheduled with the aim of matching his most valuable time—the six hours of the 10:00–12:00 block on Tuesdays, Wednesdays, and Thursdays—to the task of nurturing the firm's most important relationships. "That sets us up for success," he says.

Lunch follows these peak productive hours at noon. It's a group affair, which encourages people to take this break, often with continuing education built in. "We have frequent lunches where we stay in and watch a video together and discuss it," Hall says. There are TED Talks to watch, or someone talks about a book that inspired her. After lunch can be a somnolent time, so these hours are for activities like writing communications for clients or other activities where no one can see you yawn. The civilized ritual of teatime is observed daily around 3:30 p.m. Everyone tromps down to Starbucks, which is a few blocks away. "None of us really drink tea," says Hall. "The whole point is to get up, get the blood moving, and get out." That enables people to focus for the last stretch until 5:30 or so.

It's a very sustainable schedule. It's one that—despite growth of 35 percent per year during a time when the economy hasn't been booming—"lets us maintain some sense of balance that allows us to feel good when we go home." Things weren't always like this. When Hall and his cofounder Rick Hill launched Hill Investment Group in 2005, things "felt chaotic." With client meetings happening all over the place and no sense of rhythm, "at some level we got overwhelmed." Hall says, "We needed to get a structure—not the kind of structure that overwhelms creativity and spirit, but the kind of organization that allows us to do more."

Hall has a particular reason for wanting to monitor his energy. In 2007, at age thirty-three, he was diagnosed with chronic myelogenous leukemia (CML), a form of blood cancer. Staring cancer in the face as a young man had a stark effect on him. "What that does is give you a pretty good perspective on your life," he says. "You really get a very clear sense that there is a finite amount of time." When he came back to work, Hill Investment Group reorganized the calendar, designing each week with the goal of making work meaningful and leaving time for happiness in other spheres. "We wouldn't have a meeting, a phone call, or go anywhere with any relationship if it didn't create any energy back to us," he says. "We are picky and selective and serious about that."

Because CML is now treatable with a class of drugs that includes Gleevec, Hall can expect to live a relatively normal life. In other words, his time is no more limited than it is for the rest of us. The difference is that Hall can see this more clearly than other people. He sometimes fields jokes from friends who drive past him and his colleagues all enjoying the afternoon sunshine on the way to Starbucks. "I think people associate hard work with sitting in a workplace crunching the numbers, but we don't see it that way. We don't view activity and value as connected," says Hall. "I could create a lot of activity but it doesn't necessarily mean it's doing anything for you or for me." It's just the white noise of white-collar work. Better to have work be about getting what matters done.

And if that means watching a few cat videos? So be it. Successful people know that astonishing productivity—particularly in creative fields—requires filling the pot. Pham browses through bookstores and art blogs. You could try getting a library card and checking out something serendipitous from the stacks. You could visit an art museum. You could read professional journals in related but not immediately similar fields. You could pop over to Starbucks and talk to fascinating people. That might not look like work if your definition of work equates watching a Khan Academy video on differential equations with stealing money out of your employer's wallet. But if your definition of work focuses on output—knowing that at your retirement dinner no one will talk about your daily achievement of Inbox Zero—then it all looks perfectly fine.

PRACTICE

Sarah Fisher has spent much of her life exceeding the speed limit. She started racing quarter midgets and karts seriously in elementary school and won her first World Karting Association Grand National Championship as a preteen. In 1999, the year she turned nineteen, she became the youngest woman ever to compete in the Indianapolis 500. By the time she retired in late 2010 she'd competed in that race nine times.

The regimen required to stay in peak racing form for all those years was "grueling," she says, laughing. "I'm glad I don't do that anymore!" After spending the first half hour of the day attending to the administrative work of what became Sarah Fisher Hartman Racing, the team she founded in 2008, she'd spend ninety minutes to two hours lifting weights, running, and doing other drills with the USA Diving team, which is also headquartered in Indianapolis. In addition to working out, she'd do mental training. "Our sport is so fast, you have to have very good reaction timing," she says, so she'd practice that. Then, after lunch, she'd come back to the shop to dive into any marketing or accounting tasks necessary to run her twenty-five-person small business, but also to focus on other aspects of performance improvement. With race cars, "it's not like you can fire it up and go around the block," she says, and renting a facility and running an average test could cost $50,000–$100,000 per day. So she did a lot of simulator-based training and wind tunnel tests and studied the data that came out of the race car. "Reviewing that data—how the car rides on the road, how it rolls, different displacement—that gives you really good feedback," she says. If you decipher that, "you can figure out changes to make next time."

Judging from her schedule, it seems Fisher spent around half her time as a professional driver actively trying to get better at her job. The professional musicians I've interviewed over the years develop similar schedules. Even as they face e-mail barrages, travel woes, and demands from their PR reps to have breakfast with reporters, they are still there at the piano, with the violin, or singing scales for hours each day. Obviously, there's something to the old joke about how you get to Carnegie Hall.

Most people have no intention of playing on that historic stage or driving in the Indianapolis 500. Yet, if you think about it, your job is likely a performance of sorts, too. And you, too, would take your career to a new level if you spent time every day trying to improve at the tasks associated with your job.

Practice is, simply, performing or working at something repeatedly to become proficient. We do a lot of things repeatedly but seldom with the goal of improving. Unlike Fisher, "we drive almost every day, but we rarely get better at driving," says Doug Lemov, managing director of Uncommon Schools and coauthor with Erica Woolway and Katie Yezzi of the *Practice Perfect* book mentioned in the section on planning. "The economy is full of tasks like that. Mammographers get better when they start the job, but after the initial improvement at the job, they totally flatten, or even get worse." It's often the same with teachers—something Lemov knows from training ten thousand of them over the years—with salespeople who go on autopilot, or with scientific researchers. "Think about the social and economic cost of the failure to get better—of repeating every day, but not practicing. It's kind of dizzying."

Anything that involves skill can be practiced and, if you'd like to become better and more efficient at what you do, probably should be practiced. The best kind of practice—the "deliberate practice" identified by Anders Ericsson, Ralf Krampe, and Clemens Tesch-Romer in their famous 1993 *Psychology Review* paper on the schedules of elite musicians—ideally involves immediate feedback on one's performance and a high volume of repetition to shore up specific skills.

Take writing. The red pen gets a bad rep. You can improve at writing by having people critique your prose and then revising with those edits in mind. Sure, receiving that criticism can be painful, but it's how you learn and get better. Over time, you can serve as your own critic ("What is my point? Do I come out for it or against it? Can I say this in fewer words?"). In a pinch, a machine can help. In his essay "Structure" for the January 14, 2013, *New Yorker*, John McPhee describes using the "All" command in the text editor program Kedit to show how many times he's used "the legions of perfectly acceptable words that should not appear more than once in a piece of writing." These are words like "expunges" or "ameliorate," he notes, which McPhee then expunges to ameliorate his prose. To increase the volume of your writing, you can keep a blog or a daily journal. The higher the volume you require of yourself, the more efficient you will become. In three years of writing six to seven posts per week for my various blogs, I have probably doubled my speed in cranking out five-hundred-word persuasive essays. The posts may not be perfect now, but they're certainly better than they were the first time I figured out where the "publish" button was on WordPress.

Or consider public speaking. The best speakers are not necessarily gregarious individuals. They're simply well-practiced sorts who've honed their material to the point where they know what people will react to and they've learned to manage that reaction. Negotiating can be practiced. Cold-calling can be practiced. Meetings can be practiced, particularly those in which you might encounter hostile questioning. Anything that happens live, that you can't do over again, is ripe for practicing, says Lemov. "I couldn't imagine going into a performance review and wasting that opportunity by not practicing beforehand," he says.

If you're not sure which skills you can practice, try polling your coworkers on which skills they think matter in your line of work. Start with the most frequently mentioned one first. What is the standard of excellence for that skill? How can you practice to get better?

The employees of Hill Investment Group build practice into their days through a culture of constant feedback. "If we had a meeting with you, and you were considering hiring our firm, after you'd leave we'd gather and ask 'What did we do well?' and 'What do we need to fix in presenting our story or message, listening, or asking better questions?'" Hall says. "That can be a fragile discussion, unless culturally you have a commitment really to view it as an opportunity." Everyone is subject to feedback, including Hall. "The most common feedback for me," he says, "is to make it shorter, make it tighter, give the bullet point and then be quiet. Don't get so hung up on inspiring them to see it the way you see it."

Lemov, Woolway, and Yezzi recommend instituting drills, which are distorted simulations of reality that allow you to focus on a specific skill, just as a basketball player, in practice, might attempt twenty three-point shots in a row. If you're practicing for media interviews, for instance, you could have friends ask you potential interview questions over and over again so you can memorize how to respond. Once you memorize plausible responses, practice delivering them in a casual, spontaneous manner. As Lemov notes, "Repetition sets you free. It automates things, so your mind can think of bigger things," like remembering to smile at the television camera when the host says your name, because chances are the camera just cut to you. If your team is facing a meeting with an unhappy client next week, you might stage a mock meeting and drill the presenters with potential questions. Yezzi suggests, "At staff meetings, carve out fifteen minutes to practice." Even a little goes a long way, because people crave practice. Once you start, people want to do more. In general, people want to get better at their jobs. They want feedback and they want suggestions of what to do with that feedback.

That's what Grace Kang has discovered. Kang started New York City's Pink Olive boutiques after spending the early years of her career at major department stores, including Bloomingdale's. "I am mentally trained to look at my selling every Monday," she says. With the data in hand, she can improve her own performance as a curator, experimenting with new product mixes, like a larger paper and home decor section, for instance, after her reports showed that these products moved fast. She also carves out time to get on the phone with her designers to share the data on "what's working, what's not working." Curiously, Kang reports that these designers, who may sell through multiple channels, often don't hear back from customers. "Offering that feedback to our designers is invaluable to them," Kang says. "My manager and I spend a lot of time really educating them about what sells. If something is doing well by another designer, we really do share that with our designers, so they can act on it and create something special for us," she says. "It's time-consuming, but the return is huge."

You may not be able to devote half your workdays to improving your skills and your team's skills, but given how massively most people underinvest in this discipline, turning practice into a daily activity "will make people better at their work," says Lemov. That "is a fundamental competitive advantage."

PAY IN

I collect old magazines. My habit was greatly aided when I found a company, PastPaper.com, headquartered in Gap, Pennsylvania, near Lancaster, which offers roughly 1 million consumer periodicals, dating from 1835. PastPaper.com regularly ships me issues of *Good Housekeeping*, *Forbes*, and the like, as do some of my editors, electronically, from their own archives now that I've made my fascination known. As I crack open the covers or scroll through the scanned files, I am, for an hour, looking at history through the eyes of people who lived at that time. The ubiquitous trend pieces, unfiltered by hindsight, can show, very clearly, just how much certain things have changed.

Take how people think about and build their working lives. In 1956, *Fortune* magazine ran a story by Herrymon Maurer called "Twenty Minutes to a Career." Maurer wrote, "This month of March, 1956, will be the most hectic month in the biggest year of college-senior hiring in U.S. business history." Of "this year's crop of over 200,000 men graduates, the great majority of them will eventually go into business." (As I wrote in a piece for Fortune.com on Maurer's article, women earned

132,000 of the 379,600 U.S. bachelor's degrees conferred in 1956, but their career choices were apparently of less concern.*) American business was scaling up, and Sears, Roebuck would be recruiting 500 men, GM was aiming for 2,000 men, and GE wanted to hire 2,500. It was all very exciting, but there was inherent tension because, as Maurer wrote, the basic contact between companies and students would be a twenty-minute interview. Students needed to understand that, "for a great many of them, a brief interview will settle their careers for life." Yes, the young men who planned to work for large corporations should "consider a job offer in terms of a lifetime career." To be sure, "some large companies will hire men two or three years out of school, and a few will take them even after five years. But almost all of them hold to the policy of promotion from within." And so "for the bulk of the men who aspire to a big-business career—and for the bulk of the companies hiring them—the year of college graduation is the year of decision."

Except that it wasn't. The men from the class of 1956 would generally have retired in the late 1990s. But nowhere near all of them would have retired from the corporations that hired them forty years earlier, most notably because many of the companies Maurer wrote about no longer existed in anything resembling their 1956 form. Steel company Jones & Laughlin, which was recruiting at thirty-five colleges, merged with Republic Steel in 1984 to form LTV Steel, which then filed for

---

* http://management.fortune.cnn.com/2012/07/20/fortune-1956-20 -minutes-to-a-career-or-not/

bankruptcy in 2000. Two railroads, the Pennsylvania and New York Central, told *Fortune* they were eager to bring aboard men from the class of 1956. But by 1968 the rivals had become one company, which went bankrupt in 1970. Beyond the usual winds of Schumpeter's gale, corporate America became less enamored with the policy of promoting exclusively from within. From 1995 to 2012, search firm Crist Kolder Associates calculated, 39 percent of CFOs and 20 percent of CEOs at S&P 500 and Fortune 500 companies were external hires. While that means the majority were still internal, Heidrick & Struggles calculated that among Fortune 500 CEOs appointed internally, the average tenure with the company was sixteen years. Since the average age at appointment was fifty, this means that the majority spent the first part of their careers elsewhere. Professionals have reacted rationally to decades of layoffs by becoming quite willing to change organizations for better opportunities. According to one recent Kelly Services survey, more than four in ten American workers consider themselves free agents, as opposed to, I suppose, former *Fortune* editor William Whyte's Organization Men.

What all this means is that it is no longer sufficient to be employed—one must remain employable. That means monitoring that excellent concept of *career capital*. Career capital is a convenient way to think about the sum total of one's experience, knowledge, network, and personality characteristics. When your career capital level is high, you can cash in your chits at any point for a new situation, to take your career to a new level, or even to take a break without destroying your ability to earn a living. Successful people develop the discipline of paying in to this account every day.

These deposits take many forms. If practicing is about getting better at the skills you currently have, paying in is about figuring out what skills and knowledge you will need in the future. When you come across technical concepts you are unfamiliar with or new styles of drawing, do you write them down and make time to research them? At conferences, do you attend sessions on topics you've mastered or do you stretch to take in something new? For that matter, are you going to professional development events? Can you take a class on that topic that your boss keeps mentioning? Can you find a mentor who will help you figure out what skills and concepts you should be learning for success five years, ten years, or twenty years down the road?

The deposits can also take the form of creating a visible portfolio. The good thing about writing or illustrating books is that they are then out there in the market, speaking for you and your ideas even when you're not around. That's why experts in all sorts of fields (think medicine, politics, or business) write books or articles for industry publications, though, of course, writing isn't the only way to create a portfolio. Any sort of tangible evidence of what you've done will do, and this bias toward visible outcomes is not a bad mind-set to have. Think through your projects with the goal of having a measurable or tangible result. It is one thing to have a sense that your employee engagement program at the department store you manage is making people happier. It is quite another to document that turnover is 30 percent lower than at comparable stores. Could you pin something on a bulletin board (or

Pinterest) and say "I did that"? If so, that's another big deposit in your career capital account.

And finally, the best way to pay in is to build up a network of people who are loyal to you. One of the harshest parts of losing a job is realizing how many people were loyal to your organization or your position, not to you as a person. But if you develop the discipline of paying in right, this need not be the case. The key is to realize that people—though occasionally inefficient—are a good use of time.

Sarah Fisher, the race car driver, started the transition from competing to team ownership in 2008 and retired from racing in 2010. Now, as a full-time business owner, she's putting the lessons learned from racing into day-to-day management. She calls racing "a roller-coaster sport" because of its severe ups and downs. One moment you're winning; the next you're looking at the fiery wreck of a friend's car.

This sense of victory's impermanence has led her to focus on the human side of her job, which she thinks gives her a competitive advantage. As she told me for my CBS *Money-Watch* blog on leadership, "We care about our guys' families, and our team's families, so we take the time to have a five-minute conversation, a ten-minute conversation. Wherever an employee is, we'll say hello and spend a couple of minutes with them."* This isn't always easy, because as the public face of her company, she has to make numerous appearances and meet with the sponsors who are key to financing an extremely expensive sport. But she realizes that "it's OK to fit five minutes

---

* http://www.cbsnews.com/8301-505125_162-57562346/building -community-is-a-smart-use-of-time/

in." Being brusque about an interruption will burn career capital—and probably won't save much time in the long run. Paying attention and giving a person your full focus, on the other hand, puts a deposit in your account.

In a world where people no longer have the same job for life, it's equally important to make time for people outside your organization. Racing is about fans, so Sarah Fisher Hartman Racing (SFHR) is quick on the social media draw; when I wrote about Fisher's philosophy toward making time for team members, SFHR tweeted the link around before I could. Likewise, SFHR is expanding into a new thirty-eight-thousand-square-foot facility in Speedway, Indiana—the home of the Indianapolis Motor Speedway—in part to bring fan foot traffic and all its distractions into the offices. "We *want* to be a part of that fan interaction and really showcase our racing team," Fisher told me. "We think it will make us a little different from our competition." That accessibility is how you become a fan favorite. "It increases our exposure and broadens our scope."

That's a good phrase to keep in mind. What have you done today to increase your exposure and broaden your scope? Anyone can reach out to someone who's immediately professionally useful. Real career capital comes from having lunch, and sharing your network, with someone who's just been fired from a job she loved. These are the moments that matter. If you have a tendency to shirk this daily discipline because life is busy, it might help to keep an actual deposit list like you would for a checking account. In a notebook somewhere, or in a private file, jot down any interaction that turned from mundane to meaningful, any evidence of your abilities sent out into the universe, any bit of new experience or knowledge gained. You never know when you might need your career capital—and maybe you never will—but, as with health insurance, you'll definitely be better off having it than not.

PURSUE PLEASURE

If I am enamored with the articles in old magazines, Cary Hatch is equally enamored with the other half of the editorial-advertisement divide. Hatch owns MDB Communications, an advertising agency based in Washington, DC. Anyone stopping by to visit will immediately have classic jingles ringing in her head, because, Hatch says, "I have, like, a hundred twenty, a hundred thirty advertising icons in my office. . . . I'm surrounded by Snap, Crackle and Pop, the Trix Rabbit, all these different things." She looks around and rattles them off. "I've got the Noid from Avoid the Noid. That guy's nine feet tall, catty-corner to me. There's the Froot Loops guy, different kinds of beer icons, Mr. Peanut, the monster from Monster.com, the Aflac duck, Mr. Clean, Ronald McDonald." She explains that "the power of branding is making that emotional connection with your audience. There are so many ways to personify a brand. There's the gecko from GEICO. When you can do a personification of a brand, people become emotionally attached to the brand." She finds that concept fascinating to the point where she has a gigantic Big Boy in the lobby. "Visually, it's fun," she says. "It gives everybody a lift."

But what really gives her a lift is that she loves her work for the work itself. She relishes thinking about an advertising campaign or brand personification and seeing her team pull together to make it take shape. As she's working at the drafting table, she says, "I'm thinking to myself, I'm putting together ads and they're going to pay me to do this!" She's always enjoyed helping people advocate for different things, a passion she can trace back to being president of the Pep Club and a Pom Pom in high school and college. "To get compensation for something you love was like a big epiphany for me," she says. It's what makes her long hours possible. It's what makes her not mind that she once walked around with a new client's files in her purse for two days because they kept missing each other by phone and she wasn't sure she'd be able to pull up the notes on her phone in a convenient way when they managed to connect. As she puts it, "I can't imagine what it would be like to live for the weekend."

This is the key insight that successful people have about how they spend their working hours—an insight often missed in stories on great places to work that belabor the countervailing perks of free M&M's and an on-site gym, and also missed in the curmudgeonly bloviation of those who claim, "You're not supposed to like it! That's why they call it work!" Successful people know there isn't any virtue gained by spending your 40–60 working hours each week doing something that doesn't buoy your spirits, but that spirits are buoyed by very specific things.

Productivity, we are discovering, is a function of joy. Joy comes not from free M&M's, but from making progress toward goals that matter to you. For their 2012 book, *The Progress Principle*, Teresa Amabile of the Harvard Business School and Steven Kramer, a developmental psychologist, analyzed nearly twelve thousand diary entries kept by teams at seven organizations. They found that when "inner work life"— defined as the perceptions, emotions, and motivations people express as they go about their workdays—is good, "people are more likely to pay attention to the work itself, become deeply engaged in their team's project, and hold fast to the goal of doing a great job. When inner work life is bad, people are more likely to get distracted from their work . . . , disengage from their team's projects, and give up on trying to achieve the goals set before them." So what creates a great inner work life? Analyzing the diaries, which included ratings of the subject's mood and motivation, Amabile and Kramer found that the best days were characterized by progress, with 76 percent of the diary entries from the top-scoring days featuring small wins, breakthroughs, forward movement on projects, and goal completion. Such progress was far more likely to be evident on the best days than what one might think of as important factors, such as encouragement from a boss. The worst days were highly likely to contain setbacks to that progress— more so than obvious toxins like an insult from a coworker. As Amabile and Kramer write, "making headway on meaningful work brightens inner work life and boosts long-term performance. Real progress triggers positive emotions like satisfaction, gladness, even joy."

It is this idea of making progress—progress you can see toward a completed and delightful story—that makes illustrating children's books so satisfying. You can see progress in creating ads that raise the profile of an organization you admire. "We're doing this thing with the International Spy

Museum," Hatch says. "Fifty years of Bond villains. Who doesn't love working on a campaign for the spy museum?" But these obviously fun sorts of work are not the only way one can tap into this mode that makes joy and productivity possible. Amabile and Kramer quote near-ecstatic diary entries from a software team called in over a holiday weekend to come up with the data necessary for their organization to settle a lawsuit. Writes Marsha, "Today our entire office worked like a real team again. It was wonderful. We all forgot the current stressful situation and have all worked around the clock to get a big project done. I have been here about 15 hours, but it has been one of the best days I've had in months!!" The only thing that matters—evident in those double exclamation points—is that the progress is toward a goal that matters to you.

Ideally, your work naturally lends itself to this sort of progress. You make time for deep work rather than coasting in the easily interrupted shallows. You can see the accomplishment of one step after another. You feel the inherent bliss in the moment when you know that success on something difficult is possible. It is the moment when the proof makes sense, when a pupil grasps the beauty of the novel you're teaching, or when an interview that pulls a thesis together makes you want to jump up and down.

If you haven't felt this way in a while, then maybe it's time to take a few of your work hours and think back to when you last took such pleasure in your work. Think about what you can do to re-create those conditions. There are likely ways to turn the job you have into the job you want, at least for a higher proportion of the day, particularly if you like your organization's values and people. Small tweaks add up over time. Successful people constantly look at their days to evaluate what brings them pleasure and what does not, and they figure out how they can spend more hours pursuing pleasure and fewer hours doing what they don't care about. Because while work hours sometimes seem lengthy, they aren't endless—and life isn't, either. The daily discipline of seeking joy makes astonishing productivity possible, because then work no longer feels like work. It feels, as LeUyen Pham put it, "really, really lovely."

APPENDIX

New Mornings, New Lives

I hope reading about how successful people manage their time has been inspiring. But perhaps you're also asking a practical question: do these strategies work in real life?

In January 2013, I asked people who had downloaded a time log from my website, LauraVanderkam.com, if they were interested in my giving them a time makeover. Several hundred people responded. Many of them then kept track of a full week for me, logging how many hours they worked, slept, traveled, did chores, played with children, watched TV, and so forth. I asked them what they liked about their schedules, what they wanted to do more of, and what they wanted to clear off their plates. We brainstormed some solutions together, looking in particular at how better mornings might make for better schedules in general.

Here are the time logs of four busy people, and the ideas we came up with for morning routines and other time tweaks that would make their days go right.

Log #1: Greg

Greg Moore is the head pastor of All Saints' United Methodist Church in Raleigh, North Carolina. It's a new church, but growing rapidly, a process he calls "exhilarating and exhausting."

	MONDAY	TUESDAY	WEDNESDAY
5AM	Sleep	Sleep	Sleep
5:30			
6			
6:30	Get Up, Shower, etc.		
7	Help Get Boys Ready	Get Up, Shower, etc.	Get Up, Shower, etc.
7:30	Breakfast	Help Get Boys Ready & Breakfast	Help Get Boys Ready & Breakfast
8	Pray	Pray	Drive to Meeting
8:30	E-mail	E-mail	Meeting with Bishop
9		Covenant Group	
9:30			
10		Prepare for Worship Planning Conference Call	
10:30	Clean/Laundry	Worship Planning Conference Call	
11	Prepare for Meeting		
11:30		Drive to Lunch with Colleague	
12PM		Lunch with Nathan	
12:30	Drive to Meeting		
1	Meeting with Conference Worship Planning Team	Drive to Office	
1:30		Write Ash Wednesday Homily	
2			

While Moore has been growing the church, his family has grown as well; he and his wife, Molly (who works part-time in statistical analysis), have a three-year-old and a one-year-old. Here's what a week in early 2013 looked like for him.

THURSDAY	FRIDAY	SATURDAY	SUNDAY
Sleep	Sleep	Sleep	Sleep
			Get Up, Shower, etc.
Get Up, Shower, etc		Breakfast	Prepare for Worship
Help Get Boys Ready & Breakfast	Breakfast		
Pray		Play with Boys	
	Play with Boys		
E-mail		Clean/Chores	Drive to Church
Sermon Writing			Prepare with others
	Run Errands with son		
		Run Errands	Lead Worship
		Hike with Family	
	Work Out		
	Lunch with Family	Lunch with Family	Lunch with Music Leaders
	Museum with Family	Clean/Chores	
			Drive Home

(cont. on next page)

	MONDAY	TUESDAY	WEDNESDAY
2:30			Drive to Office
3	Drive to Gym	Drive to Gym	E-mail
3:30	Work Out	Work Out	
4			Worship Planning with Ray
4:30	Drive to Pick Up Boys	Drive to Pick Up Boys	
5	Pick Up boys	Pick Up Boys	
5:30	Drive Home	Drive Home	Lead Staff Meeting
6	Get Dinner Ready	Lead Missions Meeting	
6:30	Eat		Drive Home
7	Bathtime for Boys		Bathtime for Boys
7:30	Read with Boys & Put to Bed		Read with Boys & Put to Bed
8	Lead Common Table Meeting		Time with Molly
8:30			Lead Common Table Meeting
9	Watch TV		
9:30			Watch TV
10	Read		
10:30		Drive Home	Read
11	Sleep	Sleep	
11:30			Sleep
12AM			
12:30			
1			
1:30			
2			
2:30			
3			
3:30			
4			
4:30			

THURSDAY	FRIDAY	SATURDAY	SUNDAY
Visit with Parishioner			E-mail
		Family Pictures	
Drive to Gym	Drive to Meeting		
Work Out	Meeting for Consulting Business		Visit Parishioners
Pick Up Boys			
Drive Home	Drive Home	Dinner Out with Family	Prepare Dinner
Get Dinner Ready	Get Dinner Ready		Eat Dinner
Eat Dinner with Family	Eat Dinner with Family	Drive Home	
Bathtime for Boys	Bathtime for Boys	Bathtime for Boys	Bathtime for Boys
Read with Boys & Put to Bed	Read and Put 1-y-o to Bed	Read with Boys & Put to Bed	Read with Boys & Put to Bed
Movie with Molly	Watch Movie with 3-y-o and Molly	E-mail	Watch TV
		Watch TV with Molly	
			Read
	Put 3-y-o to Bed		
Read	Read		
Sleep	Sleep	Sleep	Sleep

Looking at his time log, I could see that Moore had some good habits. He got to the gym on occasion ("If I don't sweat during the day, I start tensing up"), but his days were fragmented as he responded to church members' crises. He often had to lead meetings in the evenings. He obviously had to work weekends in his profession, so he tried to take Fridays off in exchange—hence the museum visit on the Friday he logged—but on the Friday we talked, he was leading a funeral. A minister's time, like a parent's, is never entirely his own. He carved out several hours each Thursday to write the sermon he would give on Sunday. But he was finding no time to work on a marriage preparation curriculum he was writing, let alone the dissertation he wanted to finish.

So how could he find time, in his busy life, for those professional priorities? Like many parents of young kids, by the time Moore and his wife got the children to bed, they were tired. They used this late-night time to watch TV together. That can be a nice way to connect, but it's not as fun as a real date. I suggested he try going out with his wife regularly for a "date lunch," since that worked for their schedules. With a regular date on the calendar, they wouldn't need to log that TV time at night just to feel like a couple. If Moore cut into his TV time a bit, he might be able to go to bed earlier. That would enable him to get up around 5:30 a.m. to spend a solid hour writing before his kids got up.

I suggested he first fill this writing slot with the marriage preparation curriculum. It was a doable sort of writing that he didn't need access to a library or help from other people to complete. As he made progress each morning, he'd build momentum toward making this writing ritual a habit. Once the early-morning work shift became routine, and he finished the curriculum, he could start moving his sermon-writing time to the 5:30 a.m. slot most days. He could then use the hours he'd managed to carve out on Thursday—which had been for sermon writing—for working on his dissertation.

He liked the idea, but he wasn't so sure he'd be able to get up. "I am so not a morning person," he told me. I found myself saying "Let's talk bribery" to this minister. He told me that the smell of freshly brewed coffee had a wonderful ability to pull him out of bed. So he pledged to set the timer on the downstairs pot and to get a small coffeemaker for his upstairs master bedroom. That way, when the alarm went off, his coffee would be right there, wafting into his nostrils, and he could grab a cup before he even went downstairs. Once he was up with his coffee, he'd probably stay up.

Maybe. He dutifully bought the upstairs coffeepot and then, that first morning, slept right through it. He tried again, then reported back, "I'm in the bad habit of turning off my alarm before I even realize what's happening, and the next thing I know my three-year-old is standing at my bedside at 6:30." We decided that he needed to start slowly. Getting up early to write turns out to be three habits: going to bed on time, getting up early, and writing. He could focus on the first two habits first, before holding himself to any particular writing goals.

That mind-set shift turned out to be key. When I followed up in early March, he reported back, "Last week was actually a bit more successful." He was going to bed earlier and aiming to wake up at 5:30—which he'd managed to do on the day he e-mailed me—"with time to just be. I am finding that if I make that space gracious, rather than tyrannically trying to crank out work, I am more likely to actually get up."

Log #2: Darren

Darren Roesch is an assistant professor at the Baylor College of Dentistry in Dallas, Texas. He teaches pharmacology, physiology, and neuroscience, with an emphasis on the scholarship of teaching and learning. When we talked, he was working toward his master's degree in education for health-care professionals. He lived near his work and could walk there, and home for lunch. Here's what his schedule looked like.

	MONDAY	TUESDAY	WEDNESDAY
5AM	Shower, walk the dogs, meal	Shower, walk the dogs, meal	Shower, walk the dogs, meal
5:30			
6			
6:30	Walk to work		
7	Meditation, reflection, journal writing	Meditation, reflection, journal writing	Meditation, reflection, journal writing
7:30			
8	E-mail and to-do list	Coffee break, Internet	E-mail and to-do list
8:30			Teaching preparation
9	Walk around the block	Walk around the block	
9:30	Master's degree work	Academic writing	Walk around the block
10			Teaching preparation
10:30		E-mail, Internet	

Roesch told me, "I am currently trying to institute a routine in order to make sure I cover all my bases." These included teaching, teaching preparation, educational research, clinical research, writing, working on his master's degree, and so forth. The problem? "I'm not much of a routine person, I like to free flow." But with all he wanted to do, he didn't think a freestyle approach to his days was going to cut it anymore. He would end days without making progress toward some of his top goals.

I asked him how much time he wanted to devote to each of his work priorities. He told me that he wanted to do two hours per day of teaching preparation and one hour of master's

THURSDAY	FRIDAY	SATURDAY	SUNDAY
Shower, etc.	Shower, etc.	Sleep	Sleep
Walk to work	Coffee break, Internet		
Meditation, reflection, journal writing			
	Meditation, reflection, journal writing	Time with the dogs	
To-do List and e-mail		Coffee and thinking	
Coffee break, Internet	To-do list and e-mail		Walk the dogs
Work on revising work website			Coffee and thinking
Teaching Preparation	Daily tasks on to-do list		
		AA meeting	
	Teaching preparation		Shower, etc.
Master's degree work			Church

(cont. on next page)

	MONDAY	TUESDAY	WEDNESDAY
11	Walk home, walk the dogs, eat lunch, walk back to work	Walk home, walk the dogs, eat lunch walk back to work	Walk home, walk the dogs, eat lunch, walk back to work
11:30			
12PM			Department seminar
12:30	Phone calls		
1	Walk around the block	Teaching preparation	Neuroscience lecture
1:30	Playing on the Internet		
2		Thinking and goal setting	Walk around the block
2:30			Thinking and goal setting
3	Neuroscience lecture	Walk around the block	
3:30		Snack	
4	To-do list maintenance	Thinking and goal setting	
4:30	Journal writing		Walk home
5	Walk home	Walk home	Relax, reading, etc.
5:30	Relax, reading, etc.	Relax, reading, etc.	
6			
6:30			
7			
7:30	Meal	Meal	Meal
8	Relax, reading, etc.	Relax, reading, etc.	Relax, reading, etc.
8:30			
9			
9:30			
10	Sleep	Sleep	
10:30			
11			
11:30			

THURSDAY	FRIDAY	SATURDAY	SUNDAY
Walk home, walk the dogs, eat lunch, walk back to work	Walk home, walk the dogs, eat lunch, walk back to work	Errands	
	Department seminar	Reflection and journal writing	
Tea break, Internet			
Conference call	Thinking and goal planning	Walk the dogs	AA meeting
		Hair cut	
			Errands
Thinking and goal setting			
		Chores	
Journal writing	Plan next week goals		Reflection and journal writing
Walk home and relax	Walk home		Nap
Read	Relax, reading, etc.	Relax, reading, etc.	
			Reading, relaxing, etc.
	Dinner out		Weekly to-do list, etc.
Meal			
Playing on Internet			Meal
Sleep	Sleep	Sleep	Sleep

(cont. on next page)

(cont. from previous page)

	MONDAY	TUESDAY	WEDNESDAY
12AM			
12:30			
1			
1:30			
2			
2:30			
3			
3:30			
4			
4:30			

degree work. He said he wasn't doing a good job of protecting "sacred writing time. Ideally, I would have two blocks of writing time: one block for academic writing and one block for Internet/blog writing. At least an hour for each." He'd start the day with good intentions—indeed, he was an early riser and started work quite early with his journaling—but "I do a lot of Internet surfing," he said. "Many of the long coffee and tea breaks are periods spent surfing the Internet and checking e-mail." He wanted suggestions on reining that in.

In theory, four blocks of one to two hours each could be doable. Roesch didn't have kids, and he told me that there was nothing preventing him from working late. But when people start their days at 5:00 a.m., they often find it hard to do intense thinking at 7:00 p.m. I'm also wary of packing days too tightly—a problem I've seen in many corporate logs featuring seven hours of meetings in a day. Things come up, and if you have seven intense hours already spoken for, you won't have space to react to problems or seize opportunities. A better approach might be to try to do four one-hour blocks and see how that went.

THURSDAY	FRIDAY	SATURDAY	SUNDAY

Of his four priorities, Roesch identified academic writing as his biggest challenge, with teacher prep as a close second. Since he was clearly a morning person, I suggested he tackle his toughest work as soon as he sat down at the office, while his mind was still fresh.

Here's the schedule we came up with together:

> 7:00–8:00 academic writing
> 8:00–8:20 quick walk, grab a coffee, *don't check e-mail*
> 8:20–9:20 teaching preparation
> 9:20–9:45 quick walk, take a look at e-mail, but only answer urgent things
> 9:45–10:45 Internet writing

He tended to take an early lunch, leaving the office by 11:00 to walk back to his house to let the dogs out. He'd be back at work by noon.

Roesch often had some sort of meeting after that or he'd teach classes then or he'd be dealing with students. I suggested he look at his schedule before the week started and figure out where he could block in one hour each afternoon for his master's degree work. If he was working until 5:00 or so, he just had to figure out one hour of the five-hour block between 12:00 and 5:00. That would leave plenty of time for catching up with things. Knowing he'd already hit three of his top four priorities by lunch, he'd be more relaxed and open to dealing with the distractions that came his way.

He reported back after a few weeks. "I have been using the general schedule. I spend an hour on writing. I take a walk around the block. Then I do an hour on teaching prep and take another walk. For the third hour of the morning, I found that I had to do a second hour of teaching prep because I had a deadline to get some handouts ready for an upcoming series of lectures." He'd finished up those lectures, though, so he was hoping to get back to the schedule as planned, though he was debating the importance of an hour for keeping up his Internet presence and was working with a career coach on this matter.

He was enjoying his walking breaks. "I find this really helps clear my head and it seems to increase my overall productivity." Likewise, scheduling his academic writing for first thing in the morning was also a major boost: "I have already been able to submit a manuscript that I was sitting on, and I have moved on to another project."

I had suggested he end the day with journaling, instead of starting the morning that way. I'd suspected that when he started the workday with this more pleasant form of writing, he lost intensity for tackling the academic papers on his docket. Roesch was not so sure about this, worrying that he'd fail to get to his journal if he didn't do it first. He worked out an arrangement in which his partner would take over the care of the dogs in the morning, so Roesch could get to the office earlier and spend time on the journal before his new schedule's 7:00 a.m. start time. However, he sent me an e-mail later that week, confessing, "I may have to abandon the thought of doing my journal writing/reflection before my academic writing and return to your original suggestion. Today I had trouble converting back into writing after I started doing the fun reflecting."

What we do first matters. As Roesch came to recognize the value of having a routine, he reported that he had started to resist booking meetings in the morning in order to protect this productive time. "I think the walks and the schedule help with my energy and forward momentum," he said.

Log #3: Jackie

Jackie Wernz is an attorney at a small firm in Chicago. Her husband, Matt, is also an attorney, and the two of them have a one-year-old son. Blending parenthood with two more-than-full-time jobs has made life quite busy. As Wernz put it, "It's been a real challenge finding the time to do the things I used to love"—including working out, reading, spending time with friends, and getting involved in the Chicago community. Here's what her schedule looked like.

	MONDAY	TUESDAY	WEDNESDAY
5AM	Sleep until 6:30 (give baby bottle at 5:30/6)	Sleep until 6:50 (Matt gives baby bottle at 5:30/6)	Sleep until 6:50 (Matt gives bottle at 5:30/6)
5:30			
6			
6:30	Sleep/shower		
7	Get ready/Get baby up	Get ready until 7:10	Get ready until 7:10
7:30	Feed baby, breakfast with Matt and baby, e-mails to work to let them know baby is sick and I'm working from home	Internet until 7:30	Visit with baby and Matt until 7:20; drive to work
8	Work from home (8 a.m. until 4:15 p.m—billed 7 hours: 2 hours to my own business development work; .8 hours to a partner's business development work, and 4.2 to client work/my billable minimum), tended to baby and ate lunch when not working (Matt was at home on a full "sick day" so he handled the major baby duties); 4:15–4:45 play with baby	Get baby up, feed baby, get baby stuff ready for nanny, listen to NPR and talk with baby about it while doing all of the above	Work
8:30		8:15 leave for work	
9		Work	
9:30			
10			

THURSDAY	FRIDAY	SATURDAY	SUNDAY
Sleep until 6:20 (give baby bottle at 5:30/6)	Sleep until 6:20 (Matt gives baby bottle at 5:30/6).	Sleep until 7:30 (give baby bottle at 5:30/6).	Sleep until 7 (give baby bottle at 5:30/6)
Get ready until 7:00	Get ready until 7:10		
Take dog to daycare; drive to work	Drive to work, in a 7:30		Get baby up, feed baby breakfast, get ready for church and get baby ready for church until 8:15
Work	Work until 4:15; drive home, home at 4:30	Make breakfast for Matt and me while Matt feeds baby breakfast, visit, eat together	
		Get ready to leave house (15 min); go out for walk until 9 with Matt, baby, and dog	At 8:15, walk to church with Matt and baby, stopping for coffee and breakfast on the way
		Internet until 9:15; leave for therapy, home at 10:30	Church (until 10), then walk home (until 10:15)
			From 10:15–11 Internet (potty training and ASL research for baby)

(cont. on next page)

	MONDAY	TUESDAY	WEDNESDAY
10:30			
11			
11:30			
12PM		Lunch with junior lawyer interested in education law	
12:30			
1		Work and cab home (8:45–9 p.m.)	
1:30			
2			
2:30			
3			
3:30			
4			
4:30	4:45–5:30 work out		
5			Drive home, let dog out, change clothes

THURSDAY	FRIDAY	SATURDAY	SUNDAY
		Make grocery list with Matt; get baby up and give him a snack	Get ready for gym
			At 11:15 leave for gym
		Grocery store with baby	Gym
Lunch with female associates			
		Feed baby lunch and put away groceries	Eat lunch with Matt and baby, play with baby
Work until 4:15; leave to pick up dog at daycare; home at 5:00		Play with baby and watch end of basketball game with Matt	
		Internet	Shower (15 minutes); work on blog entry for work
		Get ready for gym/ download podcasts (until 2:20)	
		Drive to/from and workout at gym	
		Watch end of movie	Play with baby
		Shower, snack, Internet	Playdate with friend and her baby
		Play with baby, feed baby dinner, bath, get baby ready for bed, play and clean up clothes in his room (until 6:15)	
Play with baby, feed him dinner, and get him ready for bed (bath)	Visit with the nanny and play with baby; feed baby dinner		

(cont. on next page)

	MONDAY	TUESDAY	WEDNESDAY
5:30	Prep dinner while chatting with Matt, who was playing with the baby, and texting with girlfriends		Feed baby dinner, play with baby (10 min. phone call with my mom while playing)
6	Get baby ready for dinner, bedtime routine		
6:30	Cook dinner and write thank-you cards for baby's first birthday		Get baby ready for bed, bedtime routine, clean up while Matt puts baby to bed
7			Bath/read fashion magazine
7:30	Shower/finish dinner		Read online and talk to Matt; dinner with Matt
8	Dinner with Matt		
8:30			Watch 2 TV shows with Matt while organizing e-mails for work and organizing baby photos for photo album (until 10:15)
9	Watch 1 TV show with Matt	Eat dinner (cooked by Matt) and talk to Matt	
9:30			
10	Read for pleasure	Clean up (15 min); read for pleasure (30 min) then sleep	Read for pleasure (10:15–10:__)

THURSDAY	FRIDAY	SATURDAY	SUNDAY
	Another baby, F, comes over for babysitting swap (his mom leaves), play until 6:30 when Matt gets home		
		At 6:15 friend comes over for dinner, play with baby and put him to bed, help prep dinner while catching up, eat dinner, visit	
Dinner with girlfriend	Put F down for bed, then our baby; plan baby shower for a friend, Gwen; buy baby shower gifts online and chat with Matt while he cooks dinner		Cook dinner
			Dinner with Matt
	In-home date night! Rent movie and eat dinner at the coffee table		
			Watch 1 TV show (2 hours) with Matt
		Watch 1 TV show with Matt	
Visit with Matt, read for pleasure			Read for pleasure

(cont. on next page)

(cont. from previous page)

	MONDAY	TUESDAY	WEDNESDAY
10:30	Sleep		Sleep
11		Sleep	
11:30			
12AM			
12:30			
1			
1:30			
2			
2:30			
3			
3:30			
4			
4:30			

I was impressed with some of the creative ideas Wernz and her husband had come up with. The Friday-night baby swap gave both them and the other family a chance for a night out without the cost of babysitting every other week, and since the babies didn't need much attention after 7:30, Wernz and her husband could do an in-home date night when it was their turn to cover. She also got together with friends on the weekend and had fit in time to mentor a young lawyer and network with female associates at her firm.

Keeping track of her time in her whole life—not just in her professional life, which lawyers are used to doing—helped Wernz see even more opportunities, particularly in the morning.

"Our baby wakes up between 5:00 and 6:00 to eat a bottle," she said. "I had been giving him a bottle and then going 'back

THURSDAY	FRIDAY	SATURDAY	SUNDAY
Sleep	Chat with mom of other baby when she comes to pick him up, get ready for bed	Sleep	Sleep
	Sleep		

to sleep' but what I realized was that I wasn't really getting any more sleep." In fact, she said, "I felt more groggy after half sleep interrupted by the snooze button when my alarm went off at 6:00." Since she wasn't getting out of bed until after 6:00, she wasn't spending any time getting ready. "I felt ugly/awful at work every day with wet hair in a bun, no makeup, uninspired outfits," she wrote in an e-mail.

The only time she'd worked out during the workweek, according to her time log, was on Monday, because the baby had been sick, so she'd worked at home. Because she'd skipped the commute, she had time to do a workout video. But telecommuting wasn't going to work regularly for her at this point in her life, so she wanted another way to make exercise happen beyond the weekend (when she went to the gym twice).

Her solution? "This week I have been getting up by 6:00 at the latest so that I could have time to get ready (hair, makeup, clothes) and at 5:30 two days a week (Monday and Wednesday) to go to the gym. I got ready at the gym and then went to work right after." All this was a work in progress, but, she said, "I think it will help a lot if I can keep up the morning routine and go to the gym twice during the workweek, too."

Getting up without an hour of interrupted sleep, and starting the day without rushing, was giving her a new perspective on her time. "It felt good to 'find' an extra five or so hours by waking up earlier this week. It really didn't mean any less time with my son since I usually leave before he's up anyway, but meant I could get a few more things done during the week."

Having that extra time turned out to be helpful when work got very busy a few weeks after she'd logged her time for me. "Because I was used to getting up at 5:30 I just started going

	THURSDAY 1-31	FRIDAY 2-1	SATURDAY 2-2
5AM	Sleep	Sleep	Sleep
5:30	Sleep	Sleep	Sleep
6	Sleep	5-y-o up, get him	Sleep
6:30	Sleep	Sleep	Sleep
7	Wake up, cuddle 5-y-o	Sleep	Sleep
7:30	Cook/feed bkfst	Wake up, brush teeth	Make/feed bkfst
8	Cook/feed bkfst	Cook/feed bkfst	Eat bkfst, talk with friend
8:30	Eat my bkfst, online, tidy house	Cook/feed breakfast	Lesson planning
9	Play w/kids	Eat my bkfst	Lesson planning
9:30	Get ready for the day	Chat w/Mom	Vacation planning

into the office at 6:00 or 6:30 most days and so was still able to leave at 4:30 or 4:45 every day and get home for quality time with my son," she reported back. While her early-morning fitness routine didn't happen during this time, at least her other nonnegotiable activity—those early evenings with her baby—still happened. That kept her from going into a "total tailspin."

"It was really, really nice for me to not be super stressed out during my heavy time," she said. A calmer life counts as success, even if her schedule didn't look exactly like what she wanted.

Log #4: Jaime

Jaime Ake is a stay-at-home, homeschooling mom of a five-year-old and two-year-old. Here's what her schedule looked like.

SUNDAY 2-3	MONDAY 2-4	TUESDAY 2-5	WEDNESDAY 2-6
Sleep	Sleep	Awake - insomnia	Sleep
Sleep	Sleep	Sleep	Sleep
Sleep	Sleep	Sleep	Sleep
Sleep	Sleep	Sleep	Wake up, get ready
Wake up, shower	Sleep	Sleep	Wake 5-y-o up, get him ready
Bkfst prep	Wake up, feed the boys	Awake, brush teeth, stretch	Drive to 5-y-o's therapies
Pack for SeaWorld	Back to sleep, yay! (Greg home)	Make bed, brush teeth	at PT - work on Budget
Get everyone ready, dressed	Sleep	Make/serve bkfst	at PT - work on budget
Tidy house, load car	Sleep	Eat/dishes/e-mail	at speech - browse online
Drive to SeaWorld	Sleep	Music/read stories to boys	at speech - browse online

(cont. on next page)

	THURSDAY 1-31	**FRIDAY 2-1**	**SATURDAY 2-2**
10	Play w/2-y-o	Tidy up house	Greg dressed/ready
10:30	School w/5-y-o	Get everyone ready for gym	Karate w/5-y-o
11	School w/both boys	Drive to gym	Karate w/5-y-o
11:30	Dinner prep	Workout	Play w/kids
12PM	Chat w/2-y-o's speech ther	Workout	Lesson planning
12:30	Rock 2-y-o to sleep, grocery list	Out to lunch w/kids	Lesson planning
1	Online/read news	Drive home	Lesson planning
1:30	Nap	Clean out van and shower	Lesson planning
2	Nap	Relax on couch w/5-y-o	Lesson planning
2:30	Feed kids/eat lunch	Play and read w/5-y-o	Make/eat/serve lunch
3	Play outside w/kids	Make pizza dough	Food prep
3:30	On walk w/kids	Clean kitchen/fridge	Dishes/food prep
4	Tidy house/watch *Ellen*	Assemble pizzas	Food prep
4:30	Play w/kids	Chat w/Greg	Quick trip to CVS
5	Eat/serve dinner	Family dinner	Feed and play w/kids
5:30	Family time	Family dinner	Family game night
6	Family time/mop kitchen	Play w/kids	Family game night
6:30	Family dance time/ clean up	Bath/bed/jammies for kids	Vacuum/boys bedtime routine
7	Kids bath/bed/story	Read stories to 5-y-o	TV w/5-y-o
7:30	Shower	Fold laundry	TV w/5-y-o
8	Plan Friday activities	Movie w/Greg	Vacation planning
8:30	Vacation planning	Movie w/Greg	Vacation planning

SUNDAY 2-3	MONDAY 2-4	TUESDAY 2-5	WEDNESDAY 2-6
SeaWorld	Sleep	Music/play with toys w/boys	at OT - read
SeaWorld	Sleep	School w/5-y-o	at OT - read
SeaWorld	Play with the kids	School w/5-y-o	Drive home
SeaWorld	Eat, tidy house, plan the day	Shower/get ready/dressed	Fix/feed boys snack
SeaWorld	School w/5-y-o	Fix and feed lunch	Workout
SeaWorld	School w/5-y-o	Get everyone ready, loaded up	Workout
SeaWorld	Cleaning and organizing	Drive to/at library	School w/5-y-o
SeaWorld	Cleaning and organizing	At library	School w/5-y-o
SeaWorld	Fix and serve snack	Grocery shopping	School w/5-y-o
SeaWorld	Start dinner	Grocery shopping	Play w/2-y-o
Home from SeaWorld, Unload car	Cleaning	Browsing Target w/ Mom	Read to both boys
Check e-mail	Walk w/boys	Home, unload/organize a bit	Feel sick - watch TV w/boys
Chat w/Greg and my Mom	Walk w/boys	E-mail friends and MIL	Feel sick - watch TV w/boys
Make/serve dinner	Read to the boys	Cook dinner	Feel sick - watch TV w/boys
Super Bowl w/ Family	Family dinner	Cook/serve dinner	Fix/feed dinner
Super Bowl w/Family	Family game night	Read w/the boys	Family reading time
Super Bowl w/Family	Clean	Tidy house	Tidy house
Boys bath/stories/bed	Boys bed/bath/stories	Family dance/bath/bed for boys	Family dance/bath/bed for boys
Lesson Plan	TV - *The Bachelor*	Fold laundry	Rock 2-y-o, read to 5-y-o
Lesson Plan	TV - *The Bachelor*	Hang out w/Greg	Read to 5-y-o
Upload/Edit Pics	TV - *The Bachelor*	TV and curriculum planning	Vacation Planning
Upload/Edit Pics	TV - *The Bachelor*	TV and curriculum planning	Movie w/Greg

(cont. on next page)

	THURSDAY 1-31	FRIDAY 2-1	SATURDAY 2-2
9	Vacation planning	Vacation planning w/Greg	Vacation planning
9:30	Vacation planning	Vacation planning w/Greg	Vacation planning
10	Vacation planning	Bath	Brush teeth, get ready for bed
10:30	Vacation planning	Sleep	Sleep
11	Sleep	Sleep	Sleep
11:30	Sleep	Sleep	Sleep
12AM	Sleep	Sleep	Sleep
12:30	Sleep	Sleep	Sleep
1	Sleep	Sleep	Sleep
1:30	Sleep	Sleep	Awake w/imsomnia
2	Sleep	Sleep	Sleep
2:30	Sleep	Sleep	Sleep
3	Awake w/insomina	Awake w/insomnia	Sleep
3:30	Awake w/insomina	Sleep	Sleep
4	Sleep	Sleep	Sleep
4:30	Sleep	Sleep	Sleep

When I asked Ake what she wanted to do more of, she had a fairly normal parental request: "I want to spend more time with both of my kids, doing both educational things and just playing, reading, going on walks, et cetera." What was puzzling to me was that Ake was already at home full-time with her boys. Since she was homeschooling them, they weren't even apart from her for school hours. Why didn't she think she was spending enough time with them?

The answer is a problem many parents can relate to: "When I say I want more time with the boys, I am wanting more time where they have my undivided attention. I guess because I stay at home and homeschool, we are technically together 24/7 but seldom do they get all of me." She noted, "I multitask

SUNDAY 2-3	MONDAY 2-4	TUESDAY 2-5	WEDNESDAY 2-6
Hang out with Greg, fix snack	Bath	TV and curriculum planning	Plan tmrw/bath
Sleep	Sleep	Bath	Sleep
Sleep	Sleep	Sleep	Sleep
Sleep	Sleep	Sleep	Sleep
Sleep	Sleep	Sleep	Sleep
Sleep	Sleep	Sleep	Sleep
Sleep	Sleep	Sleep	Sleep
Sleep	Sleep	Sleep	Sleep
Sleep	Awake	Sleep	Sleep
Sleep	Sleep	Sleep	Sleep
Sleep	Sleep	Sleep	Sleep
Sleep	Sleep	Sleep	Sleep
Sleep	Sleep	Sleep	Awake w/imsomnia
Sleep	Sleep	Sleep	Awake w/imsomnia
Sleep	Sleep	Sleep	Sleep
Sleep	Sleep	Sleep	Sleep

way too much, and too often at the end of the day I am disappointed in myself that I didn't carve out time for each boy independently where my phone was put away, laptop closed, TV off, and where I wasn't switching loads of laundry or cleaning one mess or another up. Sitting down to play with toy cars for thirty minutes straight is like torture for me, but I feel so happy once playtime is over and I stayed in the moment with them. I am often hurried and impatient and that is not at all how I want to be."

What Ake had discovered was that with parenting, as with work, just because we're there doesn't mean we're really there. While there's some accountability at work—eventually your boss will notice if you're just putting in your time—the goals of parenthood are more nebulous and complex than hitting a certain sales target. Consequently, it's even easier to get sucked into the at-home equivalents of the in-box (TV, housework, puttering, and, yes, e-mail). These things make you feel productive in the short run, even if they don't have much to do with the longer view.

Without the rhythm of traditional school for her boys, Ake's days were pretty wide open, except for her children's therapy appointments. I thought she could benefit from two things. First, she needed a better morning routine. She told me she wanted to get up before her boys so she had time to herself and to check e-mail and social media and to work on other projects (including household maintenance) so she wasn't so distracted during her time with her kids. "When I wake up as they're waking up, I am immediately in responsive mode and my demeanor is not nearly as cheery and calm as I'd like it to be," she said. Since she got in bed on time, I asked her what she thought was keeping her from getting up before the children, and she answered, "As far as mornings, my only answer is laziness. I love to sleep, hate mornings, and since there aren't major repercussions of just turning off my alarm and going back to sleep, I do. Then I hate myself once I'm awake at 7:30 and I am already playing catch-up."

I would never use that word—"laziness"—when describing a homeschooling mother of small kids. Instead, I suspected that the reason Ake wasn't waking up when she wanted to get up was that there wasn't anything she was excited about doing. Days sort of blended into the next. So I thought that, in addition to a new morning routine for Ake, her family could benefit from some planning beyond her homeschooling lesson plans. I suggested she come up with a List of 100 Dreams—a bucket list of sorts—that would focus on adventures she could have with her boys. These could be the usual kinds of excursions (visits to a museum or SeaWorld) or more offbeat ones (buying something of every color at the farmers' market?). Looking at her week, she could then pick two or three adventures to have in the mornings. They'd come home, and she'd do the bulk of her homeschooling in the afternoon while the little one napped. She could also have solo adventures with each of the boys by asking her mother (who lived with her) to take the other child.

Ake loved this idea. She'd read about the List of 100 Dreams concept in my book *168 Hours* and told me, "I almost immediately started one for myself, but I never thought to make one for the things I'd like to do with the boys—what a lightbulb moment!" They'd moved to a new state a few months before "and there are so many new places to explore," she said.

I checked in a few weeks later and Ake was sold on the new routine. As she wrote me, "I am so much happier! I woke up at 6:00 last Monday, Wednesday, and Friday and got myself ready, snack bags and diaper bag, etc., ready, before the boys even woke up. One day, I took them both out for donuts, which was pretty much just as exciting as Christmas for them!" On another day, she took one of the boys to the park to feed ducks, and on another day, she took the other boy to go see a play. "And honestly? It was not hard at all!" As she put it, "I can't believe I did not do this years ago. At the end of the night Friday, all of the good moments of the week far outweighed the bad and they helped me feel better about my not-such-a-great-mom moments that always marred my view of the week before this. I think having things to look forward to and getting myself up and ready early are life-changing. I am cheerier and feel less guilt. SO EXCITING!"

Wouldn't you like to feel that way about your days? We all have the same amount of time—168 hours per week—but it's what we do with it that matters. When you focus on what you do best, on what brings you the most satisfaction, there is plenty of space for everything.

How to Do Your Own Time Makeover

While everyone's life looks different, here's an eight-step process that can help most people spend more time on the things that matter to them, and less on the things that don't.

1. Log your time. The first step to using your time better is knowing how you're spending it now. For a few days, or ideally a week, write down what you're doing as often as you remember. Think of yourself as a lawyer billing your time to different projects: work (in its various forms), sleep, travel, chores, family time, TV, etc. There's a blank time log at the end of this section, or you can download one from my website at http://lauravanderkam.com/books/168-hours/manage-your-time/. You can also scan the QR code included after this section.

2. Do the math. After you've got the raw data, tally up some of the categories. How does this feel to you? What do you over- or underinvest in? What do you like most about your schedule? What would you like to change?

3. Get real. Recognize that time is a blank slate. The next 168 hours will be filled with something, but what they are filled with is largely up to you. Rather than saying "I don't have time," say "It's not a priority." Think about every hour of your week as a choice. Granted, there may be horrible consequences to making different choices, but there may not be, too.

4. Dream big. Ask yourself what you'd like to do with your time. Start making your own List of 100 Dreams with personal goals, travel goals, professional goals, and so forth. What would you like to spend more time doing? What would you like to fill your time with? You can make one master list of dreams, or make a separate list for your family—things you'd like to do or experience together. Come back to this list often, and keep it somewhere you can refer to it frequently.

5. Give goals a timeline. Write a prospective performance review—that is, the job review you'd like to give yourself at the end of next year. What professional items from your List of 100 Dreams would you like to accomplish by then? Carve out some time to write this hypothetical statement of your achievements, be they finishing the draft of a novel, getting an Etsy store up and running, landing two new seven-figure clients for your company, or staging a small museum's first fund-raising gala.

You can give big personal goals a timeline as well. Try writing next year's "family holiday letter"—that missive people inflict on their friends and family each Christmas with the highlights of the past twelve months. What do you wish you could say in that letter? Block an hour or so into your schedule to figure out what items you'd like to pull from the personal side of your List of 100 Dreams and make happen this year. Examples might include running your first 10K, joining a community chorus as a family, or traveling to Maine for a week during the summer and eating lobster twice a day.

6. Break it down. Once you've got your prospective job review, and your future family holiday letter, start breaking these goals down into doable steps. If you don't know your first step, then "research" is the first step. Running your first 10K might involve signing up for a race six months from now, then committing to a schedule of three or four runs per week until then, slowly building up your mileage. Other steps might involve buying a good pair of running shoes, checking out a book from the library on training programs, and joining a gym, or finding good running routes in your area.

7. Plan to plan. Create a weekly planning/reviewing time. During this time, look at your calendar and block in steps toward your goals. Where can those three runs happen? When are you going to go to the library and check out *Starting an Etsy Business for Dummies*?

8. Hold yourself accountable. Big dreams are great, but if you don't create space in your life for making progress toward them, then they're fantasies, not goals. Build an accountability system—a friend, a group, an app—that will make failure uncomfortable. If you've got a run scheduled for Tuesday morning, and on Tuesday morning it's twenty-five degrees out and your warm bed seems pretty enticing, what is going to motivate you to get your shoes on and go? Answer that question, and your time makeover will go great.

50 Time Management Tips

1. The truth can be tough, but it sets us free. If you have time to watch TV, you have time to read. If you have time to watch TV, you have time to exercise. If you have time to watch TV, you have time to get reacquainted with whatever hobbies you ditched when you decided life was too busy. Rather than making excuses, be honest with yourself.

2. Start small. Build a habit, then scale it up.

3. Plan something fun every day. Life is better if you've got a reason to get out of bed.

4. Don't overthink dinner. You can eat sandwiches, leftovers, a frozen pizza, eggs, or a quick salad. The point of family dinner is to be together, not to be Julia Child. It doesn't even have to be dinner! Family breakfast is a wonderful substitute for families with busy evenings.

5. The average American sleeps more than eight hours per night, but if you don't think you're getting enough sleep, try

setting a bedtime alarm, not just a waking alarm. In a world of constant connectivity, turning off the devices and turning in requires a conscious choice.

6. Figure out how long the things you normally do in your life will take. That way, you can schedule in appropriate blocks of time. If you think your commute takes thirty minutes because it did, once, at 6:00 a.m., but you normally leave at 8:00 a.m. when traffic is worse, then you are always going to be late.

7. If you've got a long list of life-maintenance projects weighing on you, try choosing just one to tackle each week. One is doable, and then you can move on. Go ahead and schedule these for the next few weeks. Then when you find yourself fretting that the kids need to be signed up for camp while you're painting the bathroom, you'll remember that there's a week for that, and it's not this week.

8. If it's possible, negotiate to work from home one or two days per week. Ditching the commute (and the suit) easily buys back an hour. Face-to-face collaboration is important for innovation, but five days a week can be overkill.

9. Realize you look great already. The difference between a forty-five-minute personal-care routine and a thirty-minute one is more than an hour per workweek.

10. Give things a home. Time spent hunting for shoes and phones is simply lost time.

11. Own less stuff. Stuff consumes time—both in the income required to purchase it and in the hours spent caring for it and cleaning it up.

12. Nap. It might not seem productive, but taking a short nap when you're run-down can make the hours after you wake up far more efficient.

13. Lower your housekeeping standards. The house will just get dirty again, but you'll never get that hour back. The laundry can wait another day or two.

14. Match your most important task to your most productive time. For many of us that's mornings, but if your most productive time is 2:00 to 3:00 p.m., guard that hour carefully.

15. Ask for help if you're confused. It's usually the quickest approach to solving a problem.

16. Make time to practice. Few of us spend many hours actively trying to get better at the skills associated with our jobs. People who do have a significant competitive advantage.

17. Run fewer errands. Order online if you can. The cost of gas and your time easily beats shipping fees. You'll survive without that extra lightbulb for a few more days.

18. Calling something "work" doesn't make it important or necessary. Calculate the opportunity cost of all recurring meetings or other commitments. Any get-together should earn its place in your life.

19. Trying to take your career to the next level? Imagine that you've achieved a major goal and a magazine is writing a feature on you. What would it say? Envisioning the story of how your breakthrough happened can help you make it a reality.

20. Make more of holiday time by having an honest conversation with your family about which traditions and recipes you most anticipate. Go all in on the things that matter. Be more judicious about things that don't.

21. Do one thing at a time. When you try to check e-mail while writing an essay, it can take fifteen minutes or more to get back into the swing of things. Multitasking eats hours. Focus until you finish and then move on. If you need to check e-mail frequently for your job, get in a habit of spending twenty minutes on your in-box, and then forty with your e-mail program closed. You can get a lot done in forty minutes of uninterrupted work.

22. Practice saying no. When you don't volunteer for something, that doesn't mean that thing isn't important. Indeed, it could be so important that you know you can't give it the attention it deserves. Suggest someone who could.

23. Being in the right job can give you amazing energy for the entirety of your 168 hours. The holy grail is finding something you love so much you'd do it for free. If that's not realistic (and it's unlikely anyone else has magically designed the perfect job for you), then focus on small tweaks you can make to turn the job you have, over time, into the job you want.

24. Broaden your scope. Make time, every day, for expanding your network, learning new skills, and sharing with the universe what you've done.

25. Celebrate victories. Yes, it's a good occasion to open the nice bottle of champagne. What are you saving your energy—and the champagne—for?

26. People are a good use of time. Take a moment to say hello and smile and give people your full attention. It can take hours to buy back the goodwill burned in a two-second glance at your phone while someone is trying to tell you something important.

27. Micromanagement is inefficient. If you can't trust the people who work for you, you need to address that issue head-on, instead of asking to be cc-ed on every e-mail.

28. Create open swaths of time when you can. If you need to schedule two meetings on one day, put them back-to-back if possible, in order to minimize the small chunks of time between events that are hard to use well.

29. That said, if you do wind up with small bits of time in your schedule frequently, see if you can use these bits of time for "bits of joy." Make two "bits of joy" lists: one of activities you love that take thirty to sixty minutes, and one of activities you love that take less than ten minutes. That way, if you wind up with ten minutes between calls, you'll quickly pull up www .poetryfoundation.org and read some verse, rather than hitting refresh on your in-box (again).

30. Unplug. Earth will not crash into the sun if society is starved of your input for a few hours. Set limits for yourself: no smart-phone usage before 7:30 a.m., for instance, or after 10:00 at night.

31. Measure what you want to change. If you want to read more to your kids, keep track of this category of time, specifically. Knowing you'll need to write this down, you may be more in-clined to pick up that second storybook.

32. If you find yourself unable to focus, take a break—a real one.

33. Get outside. According to one UCLA time study, adults in dual-income, middle-class families spend less than fifteen min-utes per week in their backyards doing leisure activities. Chil-dren spend less than forty minutes. Why are you paying for that real estate if you're not enjoying it?

34. If you find yourself scheduling lots of sports practices and les-sons for your kids, try scheduling some for yourself, too. Adults, just like kids, can benefit from exercise and meeting new people.

35. Look for ways to improve time in the car. Commuting once a week with your spouse can turn this lost time into a date.

Recordings of children's books can turn a drive to school or day care into family reading time. Great music is more uplifting than the antics of shock jocks. Plan ahead for travel time and you'll enjoy it more.

36. Time invested in training children to be independent is time well spent. Sure, it's quicker to make a fourth grader's lunch for her . . . for the first week. But after that, she gains the competence to tackle this task herself. Eventually, she might start writing items on the grocery list ahead of time. Doing everything for her cheats her of the chance to learn to think and plan.

37. This is true at work as well. Time invested in training other people is a down payment on a freed-up schedule in the future.

38. Always offer to be the person initiating a call. That way it starts on time.

39. If someone suggests getting together, and you both genuinely want to make it happen, don't follow up with "How about sometime next week?" Say (for example) "Let's do 2:00 on Tuesday at the Starbucks on 42nd between 3rd and Lex; if that doesn't work, please suggest another time and place." This saves roughly four back-and-forth e-mails.

40. Spend time savoring memories. Looking through photo albums is a great way to remind yourself of things you enjoyed in the past that you'd probably like to make time for again in the future.

41. The weekend isn't over until your alarm clock goes off on Monday morning. Plan something fun for Sunday night and you'll extend your enjoyment of your days off. Sunday night is, incidentally, a great time to host parties. No one has plans.

42. Think beyond the work dinner. Going for a run as a team can also be a great way to boost morale. A client may prefer having breakfast together instead of giving up an evening she could spend with her family. Or, if you both have young kids, you could even bond during a playdate. Not all networking functions need to involve alcohol and late nights. In many cases, you're probably better off if they don't.

43. You can make more money, but you can't make more time. If throwing a few dollars at a problem would let you enjoy your leisure time more, that's a wise use of cash.

44. If you've planned something fun, do it even if you're tired. We draw energy from meaningful things.

45. Choose the bigger life. If that zip-line tour of the rain forest canopy sounds scary, remember that it will be over in an hour, and you can recount the story until you die of boring, natural causes.

46. DVRs don't save time. Whatever time you save by skipping commercials is more than eaten up by your newfound ability to watch shows that would not have existed to you in a

DVR-less world (e.g., daytime TV if you have a nine-to-five job). The best approach is to watch TV mindfully. Choose a small number of shows you enjoy most, choose how much time you will spend watching, and when your shows are done, turn the TV off. Another approach? Only watch TV while exercising. You can watch all the TV you want, as long as you're willing to huff on the elliptical machine at the same time.

47. Look for ways to trim transition times. If you decide to do something, do it. You can lose thirty minutes or more puttering around the house, putting things away, getting distracted, and losing intensity before taking whatever action you decided to take.

48. If you dislike a particular task, time it. While knowing that unloading the dishwasher takes you six minutes won't get this chore off your plate, it will make it seem like less of a burden.

49. Embrace minitraditions. Not only does deciding to have pancakes every Thursday morning mean you don't have to think about the meal, such rituals build stronger families as you develop special things you do together.

50. Write it down. Trying to remember that great idea, or even that you planned to pick up the dry cleaning today, wastes time—and you have much better things to spend your time on.

	MONDAY	TUESDAY	WEDNESDAY
5AM			
5:30			
6			
6:30			
7			
7:30			
8			
8:30			
9			
9:30			
10			
10:30			
11			
11:30			
12PM			
12:30			
1			
1:30			
2			
2:30			
3			
3:30			
4			
4:30			
5			
5:30			
6			
6:30			
7			
7:30			
8			
8:30			
9			
9:30			

THURSDAY	FRIDAY	SATURDAY	SUNDAY

(cont. on next page)

(cont. from previous page)

	MONDAY	TUESDAY	WEDNESDAY
10			
10:30			
11			
11:30			
12AM			
12:30			
1			
1:30			
2			
2:30			
3			
3:30			
4			
4:30			

THURSDAY	FRIDAY	SATURDAY	SUNDAY

To download a free 168 hours time log for tracking your hours, scan this code with your phone.